T0311408

An Analysis of

Karl Marx's

Capital
A Critique of Political Economy

The Macat Team

Published by Macat International Ltd
24:13 Coda Centre, 189 Munster Road, London SW6 6AW.

Distributed exclusively by Routledge
2 Park Square, Milton Park, Abingdon, Oxon OX14 4RN
711 Third Avenue, New York, NY 10017, USA

Routledge is an imprint of the Taylor & Francis Group, an informa business

www.macat.com
info@macat.com

Cataloguing in Publication Data
A catalogue record for this book is available from the British Library.
Library of Congress Cataloguing-in-Publication Data is available upon request.
Cover illustration: Etienne Gilfillan

ISBN 978-1-912303-37-3 (hardback)
ISBN 978-1-912127-73-3 (paperback)
ISBN 978-1-912282-25-8 (e-book)

Notice
The information in this book is designed to orientate readers of the work under analysis,
to elucidate and contextualise its key ideas and themes, and to aid in the development
of critical thinking skills. It is not meant to be used, nor should it be used, as a
substitute for original thinking or in place of original writing or research. References and
notes are provided for informational purposes and their presence does not constitute
endorsement of the information or opinions therein. This book is presented solely for
educational purposes. It is sold on the understanding that the publisher is not engaged
to provide any scholarly advice. The publisher has made every effort to ensure that
this book is accurate and up-to-date, but makes no warranties or representations with
regard to the completeness or reliability of the information it contains. The information
and the opinions provided herein are not guaranteed or warranted to produce particular
results and may not be suitable for students of every ability. The publisher shall not be
liable for any loss, damage or disruption arising from any errors or omissions, or from
the use of this book, including, but not limited to, special, incidental, consequential or
other damages caused, or alleged to have been caused, directly or indirectly, by the
information contained within.

CONTENTS

THE MACAT LIBRARY

The Macat Library is a series of unique academic explorations of seminal works in the humanities and social sciences – books and papers that have had a significant and widely recognised impact on their disciplines. It has been created to serve as much more than just a summary of what lies between the covers of a great book. It illuminates and explores the influences on, ideas of, and impact of that book. Our goal is to offer a learning resource that encourages critical thinking and fosters a better, deeper understanding of important ideas.

Each publication is divided into three Sections: Influences, Ideas, and Impact. Each Section has four Modules. These explore every important facet of the work, and the responses to it.

This Section-Module structure makes a Macat Library book easy to use, but it has another important feature. Because each Macat book is written to the same format, it is possible (and encouraged!) to cross-reference multiple Macat books along the same lines of inquiry or research. This allows the reader to open up interesting interdisciplinary pathways.

To further aid your reading, lists of glossary terms and people mentioned are included at the end of this book (these are indicated by an asterisk [*] throughout) – as well as a list of works cited.

Macat has worked with the University of Cambridge to identify the elements of critical thinking and understand the ways in which six different skills combine to enable effective thinking.
Three allow us to fully understand a problem; three more give us the tools to solve it. Together, these six skills make up the **PACIER** model of critical thinking. They are:

ANALYSIS – understanding how an argument is built
EVALUATION – exploring the strengths and weaknesses of an argument
INTERPRETATION – understanding issues of meaning

CREATIVE THINKING – coming up with new ideas and fresh connections
PROBLEM-SOLVING – producing strong solutions
REASONING – creating strong arguments

To find out more, visit **WWW.MACAT.COM.**

CRITICAL THINKING AND *CAPITAL*

Primary critical thinking skill: CREATIVE THINKING
Secondary critical thinking skill: ANALYSIS

Marx's *Capital* is without question one of the most influential books to be published in the course of the past two centuries.

Controversial in its politics, and arriving at conclusions that are passionately debated to this day, it is nonetheless a fine example of the creative combination of a philosophical method (the dialectic) with historical and economic information to produce a new interpretation of history.

Marx's belief that he had arrived at a scientific way of describing the present and predicting the future may not be shared by many of his modern interpreters. But his ability to connect things together in new ways is not in doubt – and nor is the influence of the new hypotheses that he generated as a result of so much careful analysis of the political, economic and social problems confronting his contemporaries.

ABOUT THE AUTHOR OF THE ORIGINAL WORK

Karl Marx was born in 1818 in the German state of Prussia. As a journalist, he lost his first job when the radical newspaper he worked for was shut down. But Marx remained a controversial voice. He became an enormously influential political thinker and philosopher, co-authoring *The Communist Manifesto*, which called on the working class to create a socialist society and provided the ideological basis for communism. Expelled from various countries, Marx finally settled in London. It was there that he wrote his most famous work, *Capital*. He died aged 64, the book still unfinished.

ABOUT MACAT

GREAT WORKS FOR CRITICAL THINKING

Macat is focused on making the ideas of the world's great thinkers accessible and comprehensible to everybody, everywhere, in ways that promote the development of enhanced critical thinking skills.

It works with leading academics from the world's top universities to produce new analyses that focus on the ideas and the impact of the most influential works ever written across a wide variety of academic disciplines. Each of the works that sit at the heart of its growing library is an enduring example of great thinking. But by setting them in context – and looking at the influences that shaped their authors, as well as the responses they provoked – Macat encourages readers to look at these classics and game-changers with fresh eyes. Readers learn to think, engage and challenge their ideas, rather than simply accepting them.

'Macat offers an amazing first-of-its-kind tool for interdisciplinary learning and research. Its focus on works that transformed their disciplines and its rigorous approach, drawing on the world's leading experts and educational institutions, opens up a world-class education to anyone.'

Andreas Schleicher
Director for Education and Skills, Organisation for Economic
Co-operation and Development

'Macat is taking on some of the major challenges in university education … They have drawn together a strong team of active academics who are producing teaching materials that are novel in the breadth of their approach.'

Prof Lord Broers,
former Vice-Chancellor of the University of Cambridge

'The Macat vision is exceptionally exciting. It focuses upon new modes of learning which analyse and explain seminal texts which have profoundly influenced world thinking and so social and economic development. It promotes the kind of critical thinking which is essential for any society and economy. This is the learning of the future.'

Rt Hon Charles Clarke, former UK Secretary of State for Education

'The Macat analyses provide immediate access to the critical conversation surrounding the books that have shaped their respective discipline, which will make them an invaluable resource to all of those, students and teachers, working in the field.'

Professor William Tronzo, University of California at San Diego

WAYS IN TO THE TEXT

KEY POINTS

- Karl Marx grew up at the height of the industrial revolution.* Criticism of capitalism* guided his life.

- *Capital* analyzes how the capitalist mode of production* operates. It studies its rise and predicts its fall.

- *Capital* is a multidisciplinary work. It uses unique ways to look at the world.

Who Was Karl Marx?

Karl Marx, the son of a successful lawyer, was born on May 5, 1818, in the German state of Prussia.* The early nineteenth century was a time of rapid urbanization and industrialization,* when a new class of capitalists* and a new working class* came into being.

After earning a doctorate in philosophy, Marx took a job as a radical journalist. His criticism of the state authorities and the king led to his newspaper being shut down. Marx then married and moved to Paris where he met the German social scientist Friedrich Engels,* who shared his socialist* ideals.

Marx's radicalism meant he was soon expelled from France. The family moved to Belgium and, together, Marx and Engels wrote the *Communist Manifesto.** This pamphlet called on the working class to unite and create a socialist society.* The *Manifesto* was published in

1848,* a year in which revolutions broke out across Europe. Marx returned to Germany to edit a radical newspaper, but by the summer of 1849 the revolutionaries had been defeated. Packing up once again, Marx, his family, and Engels headed for England, where Engels's father part-owned a cotton factory.

While Engels managed his father's factory, Marx settled in London, working as a freelance journalist. The following decades were hard and three of his seven children died. However, sustained by money from Engels, Marx was able to carry on studying capitalism going on to write several books, including his major work *Capital: A Critique of Political Economy*. He died in 1883, with only the first volume of *Capitalism* published.

What Does *Capital* Say?

Marx saw capitalism as a social structure that is dedicated to producing commodities* in order to create a profit. This central goal prioritizes "things" (the products of human labor) over social relationships. Marx opposed the system and hoped his book would contribute to capitalism's overthrow.

In *Capital*, Marx studied the way that capitalism develops and grows, considering the entire historical era of capitalism from its origin to its predicted demise. He is fiery in his denunciation of the roots of capitalism: the process by which some groups were dispossessed by other groups. He shows how that dispossession took many forms, from removing peasants from the land to make way for capitalist agriculture, to the horrors of the slave trade. The enormous wealth generated by the transatlantic slave trade helped to finance the growth of banking capital in England.

Marx also describes capitalism as a system that would not last. He had two key reasons for believing it would fail:

1. In order to work, capitalism relies on the existence of two classes,

a capitalist class and a working class. The capitalists are owners, they have enough capital to buy other people's labor and use it to create new commodities. These commodities can then be sold to make a profit. The only commodity the working class has available to sell is its ability to work. Marx calls this labor power.* Capitalists buy the labor of the working class and give them a wage in return. However, Marx believed that wages did not reflect the true value of the working class's labor power. He argued that the working class created more value than it received, which he termed surplus value.* This surplus value is taken by capitalists and *not* redistributed throughout society. In effect, the capitalists were exploiting the working class. Marx argued that when the workers became aware that they were giving more than they were receiving, they would revolt against capitalism and end the system.

2. Marx argued that there was another destructive flaw in capitalism. To make profits, capitalists must sell commodities for more than the cost of production. They compete with one another to sell their commodities. If too many capitalists invest in lucrative areas, the markets in these areas become saturated. At this point, prices and profits fall. However, capitalists want to keep profits high, so they try to reduce costs. They do this by cutting wages, increasing working hours, and getting workers to work harder. They invest in new machinery to increase productivity and gain temporary advantages over competitors. However, these advantages disappear when other competitors invest in similar machines. Profit rates rise and fall, which is why capitalism moves through cycles of boom (economic upturn) and slump (economic downturn). During periods of economic crisis, smaller capitalists are squeezed out and capital concentrates in fewer hands. Marx predicted this process would go on until capital was concentrated in a single monopoly. In this scenario, capitalism consumes itself.

Marx proposes replacing the capitalist system with that of a planned economy.* In a planned economy the whole society collectively owns the means of production.*

Why Does *Capital* Matter?

Marx's *Capital* is one of the most influential books ever written. It played a pivotal role in twentieth-century world politics and asks questions that remain important today.

Following on from the Russian Revolution* of 1917, Marxist thought became the basis of state ideology when the Soviet Union* came into being in 1922. After World War II* the Soviet Union increased its area of influence, as communist states* were established in central and eastern Europe. In the capitalist West, Marx's ideas were now seen as inseparable from their real-world application. "Marxism" had become the way Marx's ideas were co-opted by these authoritarian communist states. So, when the Soviet Union and the European communist states collapsed* between 1989 and 1991, large portions of Western academic thought deemed Marxism a failure. Their response was to dismiss all of Marx's thinking.

Clear arguments can be made opposing this point of view. The first is that a number of countries in the world still adhere to Marxist ideology. The largest and wealthiest of these is China,* a country that some commentators assert is now a capitalist economy. The Chinese leader Xi Jinping,* however, emphasizes the centrality of Marxist ideology to the Chinese Communist Party and the Chinese state.

The second argument is that some commentators believe Marxism may emerge elsewhere in the world. A 2014 report by the British Ministry of Defence (MOD) included this idea. Its authors suggested that global inequalities could lead to anti-capitalist ideologies among dispossessed groups. Marxism could be amongst these ideologies. The MOD report also warns that, if economic problems sharply affect former communist states like Russia, "a return to more severe forms of authoritarianism, and even Marxism, is possible." [1]

A third argument is that there are insightful ideas in *Capital* that still have much to offer. The book often looks at familiar problems from a new perspective. As a result, its readers gain new ways of looking at subjects and disciplines. Marx investigates the relationship between the individual and society. He studies the nature of human morality. He looks at how language reflects social conflict and questions the purpose of education. In *Capital,* Marx asks basic questions about the way that people live and work and think: issues that impact on us all.

NOTES

1   UK Ministry of Defence, *Global Strategic Trends: Out to 2045,* April 30, 2014, 134, accessed March 20, 2015, https://www.gov.uk/government/uploads/system/uploads/attachment_data/file/328036/DCDC_GST_5_Secured.pdf.

SECTION 1
INFLUENCES

MODULE 1
THE AUTHOR AND THE HISTORICAL CONTEXT

KEY POINTS

- *Capital* is a critical analysis of how capitalism* works. The book had a huge impact on twentieth-century history.

- Marx dedicated his life to the revolutionary overthrow of capitalism, although he acknowledged that the system had brought progress and had undermined old forms of authority.

- Marx used scientific methods to study social relations.

Why Read This Text?

Capital: A Critique of Political Economy was the culmination of Karl Marx's life work. Marx was interested in the social dynamics that allowed capitalism to work. He called these relationships capitalism's "law of motion."*

Marx argued that capitalism was a dynamic—even revolutionary—mode of production,* but he fervently opposed it. He believed that there was an unsustainable contradiction at the heart of the system. He pointed out that capitalists were reliant on the working class* to make their money as it was the labor of the workers that created value within the capitalist system. However, although capitalists were reliant on the working class, they also exploited them. They did this by keeping for themselves the surplus wealth that the workers created, instead of sharing it. Marx argued that this imbalance led, periodically, to crises of social upheaval and unrest. He believed that these crises would lead to capitalism's eventual overthrow.

66 Marx also discovered the special law of motion
governing the present-day capitalist mode of production
and the bourgeois society that this mode of production
has created. The discovery of surplus value suddenly
threw light on the problem, in trying to solve which all
previous investigations, of both bourgeois economists
and socialist critics, had been groping in the dark. 99

Friedrich Engels, *Speech at the Grave of Karl Marx*

The German social scientist Friedrich Engels* agreed with Marx.
He became Marx's friend and collaborator, saying that the German
workers' movement* should treat *Capital* as their "*theoretical bible,* as
the armory from which they will take their most telling arguments."[1]
And Marx's ideas *were* used to justify action against capitalism. *Capital*
helped to spark social unrest, political dissent, and intellectual criticism
for more than a century after the book was written. States were
inspired by Marx's ideas: by 1987, a third of the world's population
lived under governments that claimed to follow Marx's ideas.[2]
However, in 1989 these communist* governments started to fall and
the influence of Marxism* waned. However, in 2008, a deep economic
crisis* affected much of the world. This reawakened interest in Marx's
ideas, particularly in his criticisms of capitalism.

Author's Life

Marx was born in May 1818 in Prussia,* the most powerful of the
German states. The family was Jewish and his father was a lawyer. After
anti-Jewish legislation was passed in Prussia, Marx senior converted to
Christianity in order to retain his profession. Like his father, Karl Marx
studied law as an undergraduate, combining it with philosophy. He
went on to do a doctorate in philosophy and, like other students of the

time, became interested in the ideas of the German philosopher G. W. F. Hegel.* These ideas were widely contested. Those on the Hegelian Right were conservative supporters of the Prussian state. Those on the Hegelian Left, including Marx, were critics of the existing status quo, namely its philosophy, religion, and state power.

After finishing his doctorate, Marx took a job working as a journalist for the radical newspaper *Rheinische Zeitung* (*Rhine Newspaper*). His opinions attracted the attention of state censors and the paper was closed down. Following marriage to Jenny von Westphalen* in 1843, the couple moved to Paris. Here, Marx started studying political economy*: the interplay between politics, economics, and the law. He also began a collaboration with Friedrich Engels that would last for the rest of his life. Four years later, in 1847, Marx and Engels were commissioned by the Communist League*—a predominantly German, international revolutionary organization—to write the *Communist Manifesto,* a pamphlet that identified class struggle* as the key force of history.

In 1848,* revolutions against autocratic rule erupted across Europe and Marx returned to Prussia and published a newspaper advocating revolutionary democracy. The following year though the revolutionaries were defeated and Marx and his family fled to Britain, where Engels joined them. Marx settled in London, the center of the British Empire and the capitalist financial system. Engels went to Manchester, the heartland of British production, where his father part-owned a cotton mill that Engels helped to manage. In London, Marx continued to study and write on political economy, composing the first volume of his classic text, *Capital,* between 1863 and 1867. But Marx's restless mind and obsessive attention to detail prevented him from completing the text. He worked on the manuscripts of the second and third volumes but died in 1883 before they had been finished.[3]

Author's Background

Marx was a European, whose ideas and work need to be understood in the context of the European Enlightenment.* This "intellectual awakening" took place between the 1650s and the 1780s and saw old beliefs giving way to a new admiration for reason, science, and logic. The Enlightenment helped to produce a scientific revolution that used systematic thought to explain the world. Controlled experiments were designed to test and reproduce results. The use of mathematical models helped to formalize hypotheses.[4] Experiments based on trial and error resulted in a rapid increase of inventions. The rising capitalist class* used these new inventions to increase their profits and productivity. Technical progress in one field reinforced progress in another: for example, there were links between the development of the steam engine and advances in coal mining, textile manufacture, and the cotton industry.[5]

Scientific understanding of the world challenged traditional religious power and authority. It increased knowledge and encouraged materialist* thinking. While the religious used spiritual, "otherworldly" concerns to determine their actions, materialists looked to the material world. The new bourgeoisie* played an important political role in this context. They challenged traditional authority, opposing feudal* interests and undermining the religious establishment. The French Revolution* of 1789 demanded that society be organized and governed according to principles of reason and based on universal principles of equality, liberty, and fraternity.

Marx was born at the peak of the Industrial Revolution,* three decades after the French Revolution. He was deeply influenced by progressively minded people of his father's generation, like the Prussian aristocrat Baron von Westphalen.* The Baron—who would become Marx's father-in-law—inspired the young Marx by explaining to him the socialist* ideas of the French philosopher, Henri de Saint Simon.*

NOTES

1   Karl Marx and Friedrich Engels, *Collected Works,* vol. 20 (London: Lawrence and Wishart, 1985), 201.

2   Janos Kornai, *The Socialist System: The Political Economy of Communism* (Oxford: Clarendon Press, 2007), 7.

3   See Francis Wheen, *Karl Marx: A Life* (New York: W.W. Norton, 2001).

4   Justin Yifu Lin, *Demystifying the Chinese Economy* (Cambridge: Cambridge University Press, 2012), 22–43.

5   Joseph Needham et al., *Science and Civilisation in China*, vol. 7, part 2 (Cambridge: Cambridge University Press, 2004), 63–5.

MODULE 2
ACADEMIC CONTEXT

KEY POINTS

- Marx used a revolutionary philosophy to criticize the inner workings of capitalism,* a system he believed would be temporary.

- Marx examined the social relationships that underpinned capitalism. He explored these from the perspective of the working class.*

- Marx developed new insights into the field of political economy.* He argued that the ideas of its practitioners were constrained by their place in society.

The Work in its Context

Karl Marx's *Capital: A Critique of Political Economy* was written in the aftermath of the Industrial Revolution.* New machines, commercial growth, and accelerated urbanization had brought profound—and wrenching—changes to everyday life. A school of thought called political economy sought to understand the dynamics of this new economic system. It studied capitalism, looking at factors such as the division of labor, agriculture, and economic crises.*

Capital is often classified as a work of political economy but it was also inspired by socialist* visionaries. The French Revolution* brought about dramatic changes in thinking. It raised ideas of rational social organization and popular administration, and stimulated philosophical debate on why societies and their ideas change.

Marx drew, too, on dialectical* and materialist* philosophy. Dialectical philosophy suggests that the truth can be established

> ❝ Political economy can only be turned into a positive science by replacing the conflicting dogmas by the conflicting facts, and by the real antagonisms which form their concealed background. ❞
>
> Karl Marx and Friedrich Engels, *Collected Works*

through logical argument: start with a thesis, develop a counter-thesis, and attempt to resolve the two. This dialectical approach gave Marx a method of investigating ideas and events. Materialism considers concrete objects and the relationships between real things, rather than imaginary phenomena. Marxism* is significant because it combines dialectics with materialism. Marx's dialectical materialism* argued that societies develop as a result of a clash between the opposing needs and ideas of different groups.

Marx was writing at a time when the social and economic upheaval brought about by capitalism and industrialization* had generated a search for alternative forms of moral, social, and productive organization. Egalitarian socialist thinkers planned model societies and created experimental communities where these ideas could be practiced.

Overview of the Field

Marx's philosophy of dialectical materialism grew out of his criticism of the work of the German philosophers G. W. F. Hegel* and Ludwig Feuerbach.* Hegel had studied the way in which the clash between opposites generates never-ending change. He saw history as the progressive unfolding of human consciousness but Hegel also argued that the interests of any given social group—workers or employers— were subordinate to the interests of the state. This, for Hegel, embodied the collective will of the people. Marx disagreed with this idea.

Feuerbach's materialist assessment of Christianity proposed that

God was made by man. Marx agreed with Feuerbach in many respects, but he drew a further conclusion: that philosophical speculation should be combined with political action. Marx wrote, "The philosophers have interpreted the world in various ways, the point, however, is to change it."[1]

Other thinkers had believed the same. The French philosophers Charles Fourier* and Henri de Saint-Simon,* and the Welsh manufacturer Robert Owen,* had designed experimental models of social reform and of rational and humane societies of the future. Their plans and projects inspired later socialists. Conversely, Marx did not propose any detailed plans for socialism* or communism* in *Capital*. Instead, he developed a new philosophy: scientific socialism.* Scientific socialism was concerned with assessing the world as it is, in order to show how socialism could develop from existing circumstances. Marx believed that the form a future socialist society took would depend on the specific conditions from which it emerged. Rather than being a system that would start from a blank state, socialism would evolve from present conditions. This was why Marx, in *Capital*, concentrated on presenting a systematic critique of capitalism. For Marx, capitalism was the precursor of socialism. In fact, he saw it as a *precondition* for socialist change.

Academic Influences

Marx had studied the ideas of the Scottish economist Adam Smith* and the British thinker David Ricardo,* pioneers in the field of political economy. Both men accepted a labor theory of value,* which states that the value of something is determined by the time taken to produce it. Hence, a table that takes two weeks to make is worth more than a table that takes two days.

Smith had identified the division of labor as a force driving human progress. However, he also warned of its negative consequences. He fearing that it might deprive work of all joy. Smith did not investigate the effect of another partition within the capitalist system: the division between those who do the labor and those who pay their wages. Capitalist production and ownership relations dilute labor's reward while increasing the value of rewards for capital investment, supervision, and the ownership of land. Smith and Ricardo failed to see that capitalist wealth was generated by exploiting wage-earners. Marx believed that this failure did not stem from intellectual frailty on the part of these thinkers but was the result of a conflict of interests. Since Smith and Ricardo approached economics from the standpoint of the wealthier classes, their social position formed the basis of their ideas and outlook.

Marx argued that the exploitation at the heart of capitalism means that the system will not survive. The workers sell their ability to work; this is their commodity.* It is a unique commodity because the capitalist class* are reliant on the workers' labor to create wealth. But the surplus value* that the workers create goes to the capitalist class, not to the workers. Thus a contradiction arises: the capitalist exploits the worker and is dependent on his labor at the same time.

Starting with this contradiction, Marx developed a narrative about the way capitalism will end. He imagined the working class becoming aware of their position within society, demanding change, and organizing the revolutionary overthrow of capitalism. Marx believed that this would signal an end to economic contradictions in society and the gradual disappearance of class itself.

NOTES

1   Karl Marx and Friedrich Engels, *Collected Works*, vol. 5 (London: Lawrence and Wishart,1976), 5.

MODULE 3
THE PROBLEM

KEY POINTS

- Marx wanted to uncover the law of motion of capitalism:* revealing the relationships that shape the way this economic system functions.

- Marx showed that conflicts between social classes lay at the heart of capitalism.

- Marx argues that capitalism functions by exploiting the working class.* He examines the way that capitalists siphon off surplus wealth from the working class.

Core Question

Karl Marx's *Capital: A Critique of Political Economy* has one central question: what are the relationships that shape the way the capitalist system works? His book argues that because capitalists are reliant on workers, but also exploit them, the system is unsustainable. At some point the workers will reject this exploitation. Marx argued that capitalism compels people to adopt certain roles. He compares people living in a capitalist system to actors wearing masks in a play. It is only by looking behind the masks that the truth is revealed; the truth about capitalism being that everyone is pursuing their own material interests. Addressing that, Marx wrote "all science would be superfluous if the form of appearance of things directly coincided with their essence."[1]

The premise of classical political economy* is that free markets* will self-regulate as they respond to changing demands for different commodities.* In *Capital*, Marx adopted this premise but argued that there was an irreconcilable class antagonism between the working and the capitalist classes.* This conclusion posed a radical challenge to the

❝ It is the ultimate aim of this work to reveal the economic law of motion of modern society—it can neither leap over the natural phases of its development nor remove them by decree. ❞

Karl Marx, *Capital*

idea of capitalist self-regulation. There cannot be reliable self-regulation in the supply-and-demand system if those who produce the supply revolt. So, instead of self-regulation, Marx argued that capitalism is characterized by cyclical economic crises.*

Marx's ideas were original but *Capital* also echoed calls for social justice and socio-economic transformation that were already present in the socialist* and labor movements.* The book provided a scientific justification for the socialist belief that the workers were an exploited class.

The Participants

The Scottish economist Adam Smith* argued that "the produce of labor constitutes the natural recompense or wages of labor.'[2] This is the labor theory of value:* the idea that the time it takes to create something determines its value. This was the founding tenet of the classical school of political economy.* However, the idea that an individual is rewarded for what they produce doesn't work when it is applied to the labor of a capitalist or a landlord.

There is also a difference between the value of the product that a worker's labor produces and the value of their wage. The British economist David Ricardo* acknowledged this, writing, "The value of a commodity, or the quantity of any other commodity for which it will exchange, depends on the relative quantity of labor which is necessary for its production, and not on the greater or less compensation which is paid for that labor."[3] However, Ricardo did not go on to draw any conclusions from this about the value of labor power.*

Marx argued that workers sell their labor power—their ability to work—as a commodity. The value of a commodity is the time required to produce it. The value of labor power is, therefore, the cost required to produce and reproduce the working class. It's the cost of providing them with food and shelter and enabling them to raise children.

Marx also highlighted the concept of surplus value:* the difference between the value workers add to the products they make and the value of their wage. Marx argued that the surplus value extracted from the workers is the source of capitalist accumulation, including rent, interest, and profit. He believed that this appropriation of the surplus value created an irreconcilable class struggle.* This theory provided the socialist movement with a powerful revolutionary doctrine.

The Contemporary Debate

Classical political economy explained economic phenomena from the standpoint of the owners of capital. The Scottish economist Adam Smith believed that the profits made by capitalists were compensation for their work of supervision and for the commercial risk they took. In contrast, Marx's arguments reflected the interests of the working class. This meant that both his ideas and his audience differed from those of the classical political economists. Marx's ideas were discussed primarily within the socialist and labor movements.*

In *Capital*, Marx explains that capitalists invest for profit. They invest their money by buying commodities (i.e. labor power, raw materials, machinery) to create new commodities. Selling these at a profit means they end up with more money than they started with.

Workers must sell the only commodity they own—their labor power—to earn money to live. These two classes approach the exchange of commodities and money differently. The workers sell in order to buy. Marx describes this as: commodity to money to commodity. The capitalists buy and sell for a profit: money to commodity to money-plus. Thus the capitalists accumulate by consuming the labor power of the workers.

Marx also shows how capitalists compete with one another in the market. Competition may result in price cuts or in investment in new technology. In both instances, the capitalist's profit margin falls. To increase profit, workers are exploited more: they may have their wages cut or they may be asked to work longer hours. Their additional work means that the rate of surplus value will rise.

Marx had outlined his theory of the exploitation of the working class in earlier works, including *The Communist Manifesto*,* and he had a small but loyal following within socialist circles. By the end of the nineteenth century, Marx's scientific socialism*—the idea that socialism should be based on an accurate assessment of the world as it is (rather than as socialists would like it to be)—had become a dominant philosophy in working-class organizations internationally.

NOTES

1   Karl Marx, *Capital: A Critique of Political Economy*, vol. 3 (London: Penguin Books in association with New Left Review, 1992), 956.

2   Adam Smith and B. Mazlish, *The Wealth of Nations: Representative Selections* (Mineola, NY: Dover, 1961), 63.

3   S. G. Medema and Warren J. Samuels, *The History of Economic Thought: A Reader* (New York: Psychology Press, 2003), 268.

MODULE 4
THE AUTHOR'S CONTRIBUTION

KEY POINTS

- *Capital* created a new approach to economics and prompted a search for new socio-economic frameworks for society.

- Marx opposed capitalism.* He hoped that *Capital* would help to inspire the working class* to overthrow the system.

- Unlike earlier socialists,* Marx did not just criticize capitalism on moral grounds. He used evidence-based arguments to reveal how detrimental the system was to the working class.

Author's Aims

Karl Marx's *Capital: A Critique of Political Economy* set out to investigate how capitalism works. At the heart of the system is a set of social relationships that govern the way society is organized. Marx believed that the entire structure of capitalism is based on exploitation of the workers. To give a clear overview of how this happens, he explores how capitalism emerged and how it developed. He goes on to describe how he believes capitalism will end, using factual detail to illustrate the ideas and ideologies that underpin the capitalist system. His hope was that this approach would allow socialists who were interested in understanding the world as it really is—scientific socialists*—to comprehend the true nature of capitalism. They could then explain it to the working class.

Marx's thinking combined philosophical and social beliefs with a deep understanding of economics. From this mix he created a unified theoretical method of analysis. By challenging the assumptions of

> **" An investigation into the relations of production in a given, historically defined society, in their inception, development, and decline—such is the content of Marx's economic doctrine. "**
>
> Vladimir Lenin, *On Marx and Engels*

classical political economists, Marx revealed the contradictions of capitalism. He examined these at both a micro and a macro level, using concrete examples of capitalist practice, plus detailed empirical data to provide evidence for his conclusions. At times he also employed a conceptual approach that allowed him to explore ideas about the way that a pure capitalist system might operate. He used these theoretical models to illustrate the tensions and contradictions that existed within capitalism. This mix of methodologies represented a new approach to economic research.

Marx's book was hugely influential in other arenas, too. Marx argued that capitalism could not last. As a result, *Capital* prompted a search for alternative socio-economic systems. It also motivated attempts to create new socialist societies,* first in Eastern Europe and then further afield.

Approach

Capital was not a dispassionate, academic, study of capitalism. Marx wasn't interested in simply describing a better model of society; he wanted to overthrow the system. *Capital* was a militant call to arms, addressed to the working class. Marx's analysis was based on the idea that the working class and the capitalist class* have an irreconcilable conflict of interests. They are locked in a mutually interdependent but antagonistic social relationship. Capitalists must employ workers to get surplus value.* Workers must sell their labor power* for wages. Marx defends and supports the cause of the working class and attacks the morals, ideas, and culture of the capitalist class.

Capital is a socialist book but it differs, radically, from earlier socialist works. These criticized inequality and injustice on moral grounds. For Marx, morals, ideas, and culture are not neutral, universal values. Rather, they function to support the interests of a given class. Instead of a moral argument, Marx uses a scientific, logic-and-evidence-based approach to investigate the nature of the socio-economic system. His aim is to help the workers understand how it works and how it is detrimental to them. From that he hopes to bring about its demise. Marx believed that capitalism was a necessary stage of social evolution since a socialist society* needed to be built on the technical, scientific, and cultural achievements of the capitalist system.

Contribution in Context

Capital was written to challenge the assumptions of political economy.* Marx wanted people to understand the problems of capitalism. He was committed to creating a communist* world, which he believed would emerge from the existing capitalist society but for this to happen, the working class had to reject capitalism. So in *Capital,* Marx offered a scientific explanation of how capitalism works. He described how capitalist society is driven by the search for profits in competitive markets. Marx called this automatic search for profit the "law of value."* Companies enter profitable sectors and withdraw from unprofitable ones. The competition for profit drives incessant revolutions in technique and shapes the overall economic structure.

Marx believed capitalism was a system of creating commodities* in order to make a profit. Under capitalism the ability to work—labor power—is turned into a commodity. It is valued, like any other commodity, by the average time required to produce it.

Marx made an important distinction between price and value. He said that price only *appears* to show underlying value. The price of a worker is his wages but Marx argues that what workers produce is worth more than what they are paid. His argument is that when capitalists invest in production they buy two types of commodities on the market: living labor* power and dead labor.* "Dead labor'" refers to past labor, represented by machinery, raw materials, equipment, and so on. The value of dead labor can be transferred, so the value of cotton is transferred to a cotton shirt. However, according to Marx's theory, only living labor can add new value—surplus value—to a commodity. Despite this, profits are calculated as the return on total money invested. This financial sleight of hand conceals the way in which the workers' labor is undervalued.

Marx drew on the ideas of two prominent political economists— the Scottish economist Adam Smith* and the English economist David Ricardo*—but his original concept of surplus value was the key to explaining why capitalism was unsustainable. Capitalists exploit the workers by calculating profit based on dead labor and living labor. This hides the true contribution made by the workers—the surplus value they bring to products. Furthermore, capitalists can increase this surplus value by increasing the intensity of work or extending working time. When this happens it represents even greater exploitation of the workers.

SECTION 2
IDEAS

MODULE 5
MAIN IDEAS

KEY POINTS

- Marx argued that the capitalist* system created unemployment, which in turn created a reserve pool of labor.

- Marx said that the exchange value (price) of a commodity* should be governed by the time taken to create it.

- *Capital* was written for an educated working-class* audience. It was not finished.

Key Themes

Karl Marx's *Capital: A Critique of Political Economy* says that capitalism* exists to produce commodities for profit. "The commodity is, first of all, an external object, a thing which through its qualities satisfies human needs of whatever kind. The nature of these needs, whether they arise in the body or the imagination, makes no difference."[1] This insight is an important one. Marx is saying that some commodities are created to satisfy purely imaginary, or manufactured needs. Marx also highlighted the way in which some commodities are "fetishized": although they are just the product of human labor, they become so desirable that they acquire a "magical" power over people. When objects become imbued with this aura of desirability, it helps to obscure the fact that they have been made by workers.

Capitalists own the means of production, so they also own all the commodities that are produced. Additionally, while individual workplaces may be highly organized, capitalism itself is an unplanned system—the market is not controlled. Competition means that investments flow into the most profitable sectors of the market and

> ❝ But what appears in the miser as the mania of an individual is in the capitalist the effect of a social mechanism in which he is merely a cog. Moreover, the development of capitalist production makes it necessary constantly to increase the amount of capital laid out in a given industrial undertaking, and competition subordinates every individual capitalist to the immanent laws of capitalist production, as external and coercive laws. It compels him to keep extending his capital, so as to preserve it, and he can only extend it by means of progressive accumulation. ❞
>
> Karl Marx, *Capital*

withdraw from unprofitable ones. This generates periods of expansion and contraction, of high employment followed by periods of mass unemployment. Marx says that capitalism automatically generates a reserve army of labor composed of those who have become unemployed through market fluctuations.

Under capitalism, workers sell their ability to work, their labor power,* as a commodity. This social arrangement reveals two important points about the structure of a capitalist society. The first is that workers are free to sell their labor power (they're not slaves). The second is that workers do not have the ability to make a living without selling their labor power (they have to work to survive). As a class, they are therefore compelled to sell their labor power. In saying this, Marx was not suggesting that class boundaries were rigid. Individual members of the working class could become independent proprietors or capitalists but the *relationship* between the classes was built on need and exploitation.

Marx argues that workers' wages do not reflect what their labor is worth. Capitalists exploit workers by taking the surplus wealth that workers create. This concept of exploitation is a scientific one, but it is endowed with moral force. Marx wanted to motivate workers to battle against the capitalist class* because he believed that there is an irreconcilable conflict of interests between the classes. This conflict finds expression in the battle over the working day. The capitalists seek to extend the working day and increase its intensity. The workers seek to reduce the working day and its intensity. They both feel justified to fight for their own interests. The battle is decided by force in a class struggle* between the workers and the capitalists.

Exploring the Ideas

In *Capital*, Marx explores the concept of value, differentiating between what he terms "use value"* and "exchange value."*

Use value means that a commodity has value because it is of use to someone. Linen has use value for a tailor because the tailor can use it to make a coat but it is of less use to a blacksmith. Because the use value of a commodity differs from person to person, Marx says that it cannot be objectively measured. As a result, use value cannot be used as the basis of exchange.

Exchange value means that a commodity has value because it can be exchanged for other commodities. If commodities are to be exchanged, they must have a quality in common. Marx says that this common property is abstract labor:* the time it costs to produce the commodity. So products containing higher quantities of labor are of greater value.

Marx argued that all societies must produce goods to satisfy the needs of that society. This process has to take place but, under capitalism, the process is disguised as private labor; although it is the collective responsibility of a society to produce goods, they are only produced by the working class. This process also hides the relationships between people. For example, in a capitalist system people seem to work in supermarkets solely to earn money but that obscures the fact that people need to work in supermarkets in order to ensure the availability of groceries.

For Marx, the dynamics of capitalism wholly shape society. Capitalists compete with other capitalists. This compels them to increase the intensity of work and extend working time. This places capital in a permanent conflict with labor. Marx writes, "Capital is dead labor* which, vampire-like, lives only by sucking living labor,* and lives the more, the more labor it sucks. The time during which the worker works is the time during which the capitalist consumes the labor-power he has bought from him."[2]

Language and Expression

Capital was written with an educated working-class audience in mind and was intended to reveal the secrets of the capitalist system. Marx hoped that this knowledge would help the workers to organize against capitalism.

The language Marx uses in the book is often sarcastic. He mocks the ideas and arguments used by the ruling classes, and exposes its concealed ideological content. "I do not by any means depict the capitalist or the landlord in rosy colors. But individuals are dealt with here only in so far as they are the personification of economic categories, the bearers of particular class-relations and interests."[3] He explains that political economy* deals with conflicts that "summon into the fray on the opposing side the most violent, sordid and malignant passions of the human beast, the Furies of private interest."[4]

Capital can be a challanging to read It contains many new terms and theories and is an amalgam of styles. Marx mixes empirical evidence and abstract concepts with mystical and spiritual references and literary quotations. When his friend and collaborator, the German social scientist Friedrich Engels,* saw the draft of the book for the first time he was not pleased. "How could you leave the outward structure of the book in its present form! The fourth chapter is almost

200 pages long and only has four sub-sections … Furthermore, the train of thought is constantly interrupted by illustrations and the point to be illustrated is *never* summarized after the illustration, so that one is forever plunging straight from the illustration of *one* point into the exposition of another point. It is dreadfully tiring, and confusing, too, if one is not all attention."[5] In order to help another friend to read the book Marx wrote, "the chapters on the 'Working Day,' 'Co-operation, Division of Labor and Machinery' and finally on 'Primitive Accumulation' are the most immediately readable."[6]

Some of the terms Marx uses, including central terms like "socialism"* and "communism,"* are understood in different ways by different people. This can be confusing. And to add to these difficulties, Marx did not finish *Capital.* Engels prepared volumes 2 and 3 after Marx's death. While volume 2 was ready for publication within a year, Engels continued to organize and edit volume 3 for a decade before it was published.

NOTES

1 Karl Marx, *Capital: A Critique of Political Economy*, vol. 1 (London: Penguin Books in association with New Left Review, 1992), 125.

2 Marx, *Capital,* vol. 1, 342.

3 Marx, *Capital*, vol.1, 92 .

4 Marx, *Capital*, vol.1, 92.

5 Karl Marx and Friedrich Engels, *Collected Works*, vol. 42 (London: Lawrence and Wishart, 1987), 405–6.

6 Marx, *Collected Works*, Vol. 42, 490

MODULE 6
SECONDARY IDEAS

KEY POINTS

- A capitalist system can emerge when society is polarized into two main classes: the working class* and the capitalist class.*

- Capitalists* invest in machinery and technology to gain a competitive advantage. But Marx said that these commodities* cannot create lasting additional value and so this investment eventually causes profits to fall.

- This theory of falling profits is still debated. Empirical data may be able to test the theory.

Other Ideas

There are five key secondary ideas in Karl Marx's *Capital: A Critique of Political Economy*:

1. The concentration of capital

   Marx argues, "The more the capitalist has accumulated the more he is able to accumulate."[1] In other words, wealth leads to more wealth and to more power. Marx describes how competition between capitalists leads to price cuts. In this process, small-scale proprietors are squeezed out of business and wealth concentrates in fewer hands. That concentration of wealth is reinforced by the growth of credit, which becomes a "terrible weapon in the battle of competition and is finally transformed into an enormous social mechanism for the centralization of capitals."[2] This only stops "when the entire social capital is united in the hands of either a single capitalist or a single capitalist company."[3]

❝ No capitalist voluntarily applies a new method of production, no matter how much more productive it may be or how much it might raise the rate of surplus-value, if it reduces the rate of profit. But every new method of production of this kind makes commodities cheaper. At first, therefore, he can sell them above their price of production, perhaps above their value … But competition makes the new procedure universal and subjects it to the general law. A fall in the profit rate then ensues. ❞

Karl Marx, *Capital*

2. The impoverishment of the working class

   Marx believed that capitalist development has a polarizing impact on society. "Accumulation of wealth at one pole is, therefore, at the same time accumulation of misery, the torment of labor, slavery, ignorance, brutalization, and moral degradation at the opposite pole."[4] This worsens the situation of workers whatever their wages.[5] Marx doesn't predict an absolute worsening of workers' living standards. He focuses on the position of the workers *in relation to the total wealth produced*—a relative assessment.

3. Primitive accumulation*

   Primitive accumulation is the historical process by which one class of people emerges with enough capital to employ people as workers, while another class emerges that can only exist by selling their labor power. This process of accumulation can take many forms, such as expelling peasants from the land to make way for capitalist agriculture, or by the practice of slavery. Marx showed that the enormous wealth generated by the transatlantic slave trade helped to finance the growth of banking capital in England. For Marx, primitive accumulation is "the dissolution of private property of the immediate producer."[6] In other words, under capitalism people do not own what they produce.

4. The division of the productive economy into two sectors
In volume 2 of *Capital*, Marx examined how capital moves around. He asks how an unplanned system (the market) is able to generate the correct proportions of goods. His groundbreaking approach looked at what happens when an economy produces for its needs without accumulation, then what happens when it produces and accumulates. Marx said accumulation divided production into two sectors: commodities for consumption and commodities for production. This was an original approach to economics that anticipated the work of economists in the twentieth century, particularly the work of input-output analysis* done by the Russian-born American economist Wassily Leontief.*

5. The tendency for the rate of profit to fall
Marx developed a concept called the Law of the Tendential Fall in the Rate of Profit (LTFRP theory).* When competition prompts rising investment in constant capital* (machinery, equipment), profits fall. That's because the value of constant capital doesn't change; it remains constant. Only living labor* adds value to a commodity. Marx's theoretical model showed that when investment in constant capital increases, this must result in a falling rate of profit.

Exploring the Ideas

To understand *Capital*, it's worth looking at two of its secondary ideas in more depth: primitive accumulation and LTFRP theory.

Marx discusses primitive accumulation in the last part of *Capital* volume 1. It's the most lively and shocking part of the book, arguing that the preconditions of capitalism (two classes: one with nothing except the ability to work, the other with enough capital to employ labor) came into being through ruthless expropriation, exploitation, and blatantly unequal exchange. Marx undermines—vividly—the idea that capitalist wealth is due to the hard work or superior mental ability of capitalists. Capitalists gain the wealth they need (enough to provide an independent income plus the revenue to maintain and expand their companies) through morally repugnant forms of appropriation. His work on how societies evolved from pre-capitalist forms to capitalism remains the subject of keen academic debate.

The second important theory is Marx's idea that in a capitalist system, profits will always tend to fall—Marx's LTFRP theory. Marx reveals multiple pressures within the capitalist system, but his idea of long-term falling profits suggests a force driving capitalism towards crisis. Explained in volume 3 of *Capital*, Marx called this "the most important law of political economy."[7]

Capitalism is a system of production for profit. Profit lies at the heart of the system. Each company earns different profits and has a different rate of return on their total investments. Adding the total profit of all capitalist enterprises and dividing this by the total capital invested reveals the average profit rate. If this average profit rate falls too low, capitalists stop investing, causing a crisis in which total production falls and resulting in a recession or slump.

Capitalists invest in constant capital (machinery/equipment) and living labor (workers). Marx said that only living labor can add value to a commodity and create profits. So if the proportion of money invested in constant capital rises compared to wages, profits will fall. Many factors can counteract this process. Unemployment would reduce the cost of living labor. Another alternative would be to work people harder, so that the surplus value* of a commodity rises by proportionally more than the cost of the constant capital. However, even with these counteracting factors, Marx says that the law of falling profits remains part of the system. Eventually it exerts overwhelming pressure on profit rates and causes economic crisis.*

Overlooked

In 1929, the Polish economist Henryk Grossman* drew attention to Marx's LTFRP theory. Using algebraic models he prophesied catastrophic scenarios of crisis and collapse. However, most Marxist* economists believed that the financial crisis of the 1930s—the Great Depression*—was caused by overproduction, rather than by unavoidably declining profits.

Academics have continued to debate Marx's theory. During the long economic boom of 1945–73 interest in LTFRP theory declined. In these years the ideas of the British economist John Maynard Keynes* came to the fore. Keynes saw economic crisis as the result of restrictions on effective demand. This idea, although closely related to Marxist theories of overproduction, was seen as the answer to Marx's belief in inevitable capitalist crisis.

When the boom came to an end in the 1970s, Marxist theory explained the fall in profits as the result of capitalist competition. The British economist Andrew Glyn* rejected that theory. He argued that falling profits in the 1970s were caused by rising wages and class struggle.*

In recent years an influential Marxist, the British academic David Harvey,* has described Marx's theory of falling profits as too simplistic. He says the process Marx outlines has "a key role in destabilizing everything and thereby producing crises of one sort or another."[8] American economist Andrew Kliman* and British economist Michael Roberts* have sought to defend the LTFRP theory.[9] They analyzed long-term data on profit trends in the United States and Europe and identified falling profit rates as the root of the global economic crisis* that began in 2007–9. They reject the idea that a lack of effective demand explains why crises break out when they do.[10]

When Marx was writing *Capital* he didn't have the statistical data to verify his theory but if relevant data is collected, the LTFRP theory can be tested. This may not change our understanding of *Capital* as a whole, but it could provide empirical evidence about this important aspect of Marx's thinking.

NOTES

1   Karl Marx, *Capital: A Critique of Political Economy*, vol. 1 (London: Penguin Books in association with New Left Review, 1992), 729.

2   Marx, *Capital*, vol. 1, 777–8.

3   Marx, *Capital*, vol. 1, 779.

4   Marx, *Capital*, vol. 1, 799.

5   Marx, *Capital*, vol. 1, 799.

6   Marx, *Capital*, vol. 1, 927.

7   Karl Marx and Friedrich Engels, *Collected Works*, vol. 33 (London: Lawrence and Wishart, 1991), 104.

8   David Harvey, *The Enigma of Capital: and the Crises of Capitalism* (London: Profile Books, 2010), 101.

9   See Andrew Kliman, *The Failure of Capitalist Production: Underlying Causes of the Great Recession* (London: Pluto Press, 2012); and Michael Roberts, *The Great Recession* (London: Lulu, 2009).

10 See Kliman, *The Failure of Capitalist Production*; and Roberts, *The Great Recession*.

MODULE 7
ACHIEVEMENT

KEY POINTS

- Marx developed a research methodology known as historical materialism,* which is still of use today.
- The suffering of World War I* brought Marx's ideas to global prominence.
- It is legitimate to question the relationship between Marx's theories and how his ideas were interpreted by communist states.*

Assessing the Argument

In *Capital: A Critique of Political Economy* Karl Marx set out to write a book that would educate the working class* about the nature of the capitalist* system. He adopted an innovative approach to his research: historical materialism. This means studying history through the lens of economic and social production. Marx's method still remains profoundly influential 150 years after his death.

Marx's friend and collaborator, the German social scientist Friedrich Engels,* told Marx that *Capital* was difficult to read, saying it should be organized in a more structured style. The first volume had a poor reception and *Capital* remained an unfinished work, although Marx continued to study and write about economics for the rest of his life. When he died in 1883 the manuscripts for the remaining two volumes of *Capital* were found. Engels published volume 2 in 1884 but it took him until 1894 to prepare volume 3 for publication.

Few books have had such a vast impact on intellectual life and on society. *Capital* profoundly influenced the history of socialism* and communism* and these movements were enormously influential in

❝ These days, as the global economic crisis unfolds, Marx is back in vogue. He is chic again among politicians and journalists, and Marx's prophetic foresight can be cited to support horrific scenarios of the imminent collapse of capitalism. *Capital* is a bestseller again. The appraisal of Marx's ideas has become a timely topic. **❞**

Janos Kornai,* "Marx Through the Eyes of an Eastern European Intellectual"

the twentieth century. The influence of *Capital* was mostly mediated through secondhand interpretation of its core ideas and the book itself did not gain a widespread readership. It could, however, be argued that this is true of many influential scientific works.

Achievement in Context

The first volume of *Capital* was a commercial failure. That was partly because it was not widely disseminated among its main target audience—educated working people. It was also because the academic world was generally hostile to Marx's revolutionary doctrines. The low sales led Marx to abandon work on completing the text.

On Marx's death, Engels claimed that "he died beloved, revered and mourned by millions of revolutionary fellow workers—from the mines of Siberia to California, in all parts of Europe and America."[1] This was an exaggeration but from the late nineteenth century onwards the growth of the socialist* movement produced an audience for Marxism. The working-class* movement grew rapidly between the 1890s and 1914 but it was the horror of World War I that propelled Marx's ferocious critique of the capitalist system to the center of the world stage. The misery and barbarity of the war was the direct cause of the Marxist-inspired Russian Revolution* of 1917. This revolution transformed the international political spectrum and led to the creation of mass communist parties* in many countries inspired by Marx's philosophy.

Early in the twentieth century, *Capital* provided a framework to help study new developments within capitalism.* The Austrian-born Marxist economist Rudolf Hilferding* and the Russian revolutionary Vladimir Lenin* saw imperialism* as representing a new era of capitalism. Lenin argued, "Economically, the main thing in this process is the displacement of capitalist free competition by capitalist monopoly."[2] Lenin believed that the rule of finance capital and monopolies would inevitably generate wars and revolutions: "What means other than war could there be *under capitalism* to overcome the disparity between the development of productive forces and the accumulation of capital on the one side, and the division of colonies and spheres of influence for finance capital on the other?" It was Marxist* thought, inspired by the ideas in *Capital*, that launched the debate on imperialism and fertilized the anti-colonial* movement.

After World War II* the power and influence of the Soviet Union* was enhanced and communist states were established in Central and Eastern Europe. In 1949 a revolution brought the Communist Party to power in China.* This enhanced the power and influence of communist states and weakened imperial dominance of the world. Marxism had become the most influential ideology in world politics and in economics. In countries ruled by communist parties, Marx's theories became official state ideology and were at the center of the educational curriculum. Between 1989 and 1991 communist states in the Soviet Union and Eastern Europe collapsed.* In East Asia, however, China, Vietnam, Laos, and North Korea are still officially designated as communist regimes, as is Cuba in the Caribbean.

Few books have had such a vast impact on society as *Capital* and it has also had a profound impact on academic thought. History is the field that has been most influenced by Marx's ideas, but his insights have stimulated debate in every social science discipline. They have helped to shape whole areas of research, such as sociology and economic history.

Limitations

In *Capital*, Marx focused on the law of motion* of the most advanced capitalist countries. In other words, he looked at the relationships that shaped the economic system in the industrial West. Marx believed that socialism needed to be preceded by capitalism. He thought socialist societies* required the technical and organizational foundation that capitalism would provide. Although Marx's primary point of reference was capitalist England, he was not interested in assessing capitalism in a particular location or at a particular time. Marx was studying a system. Although he has been accused of focusing too much on European historical development, recent research—looking at Marx's notebooks—reinforces the view that he considered capitalism to be an organic world system.[3]

Marx's disciples in less-developed countries tried to devise revolutionary policies to suit their conditions. So, they asked, what policies should socialists pursue in countries where capitalism is not developed? The Soviet politician Leon Trotsky* argued that the working class could lead a revolution in Russia because the capitalist class* there was weak. The workers would carry out the bourgeois and socialist tasks simultaneously.[4] The bourgeois tasks included creating a unified nation state and economy, introducing land reform and democratic rights, and abolishing feudal* state structures and economic power. The socialist tasks included the centralization of economic power by state or public ownership and democratic control of the state and economy. It was hoped that socialist revolutions would occur in advanced capitalist countries like Germany, as the Germans possessed advanced technical and scientific knowledge that could help the Russians. However, this did not happen.

The Soviet dictator Josef Stalin* transformed socialism in the Soviet Union. He rejected the idea that there needed to be socialist revolutions in advanced countries in order that socialists in those countries could then assist socialists in less advanced countries. Instead, he created a bureaucratically administered state based on a planned economy* (an economy in which the government determines prices, wages, production, and investment). Similar social formations were imposed or developed in all other states ruled by communist governments. It was this model of socialism that dominated the perception of Marxism for most of the twentieth century. It is certainly legitimate to question the correspondence between Marx's ideas and what was done by communist states in his name. The central question is whether the communist states were really inspired by the concepts of *Capital*, or if they distorted Marx's ideas to justify bureaucratic rule.

NOTES

1   Karl Marx and Friedrich Engels, *Collected Works*, vol. 24 (London: Lawrence and Wishart, 1989), 468.

2   V. I. Lenin, *Imperialism: The Highest Stage of Capitalism* (Sydney: Resistance, 1999), 91.

3   See Lucia Pradella, "Imperialism and capitalist development in Marx's Capital," *Historical Materialism* 21, no. 2 (2013): 117–47.

4   See Leon Trotsky, *Permanent Revolution Results and Prospects* (New York: Merit, 1969).

MODULE 8
PLACE IN THE AUTHOR'S WORK

KEY POINTS

- Many of Marx's earlier works contained early versions of the ideas that he addressed in *Capital.*

- Academics still debate aspects of what Marx was saying in *Capital.*

- Marx remains one of the most important social thinkers of all time.

Positioning

Before writing *Capital: A Critique of Political Economy*, Karl Marx had spent decades studying and writing about political economy.* In 1848,* in partnership with his friend the German social scientist Friedrich Engels,* Marx had written the *Communist Manifesto.** This pamphlet was an overview of world history presented as a history of class struggle.* *The Communist Manifesto* highlighted the dynamic role of capitalism* within society. "The bourgeoisie* cannot exist without constantly revolutionizing the instruments of production, and thereby the relations of production, and with them the whole relations of society."[1] The theories of the communists* are said to "express, in general terms, actual relations springing from an existing class struggle, from a historical movement going on under our very eyes."[2]

The *Manifesto* explains that the role of the bourgeoisie is to revolutionize production and concentrate the productive process in particular geographical locations. By uniting the workers in ever-larger workplaces they are ultimately transformed into a force that will threaten capitalism. The bourgeoisie is also responsible for centralizing political activity (the state). The bourgeois mode of production*

> ❝ His aim is to convert the radical political project from
> what he considered a rather shallow utopian socialism*
> to a scientific communism. But in order to do that,
> he can't just contrast the utopians with the political
> economists. He has to re-create and reconfigure what
> social scientific method is all about … How can we
> both understand and critique capitalism *scientifically* in
> order to chart the path to communist revolution more
> effectively? ❞
>
> David Harvey, *A Companion to Marx's Capital*

reveals that the old feudal* relations of production hinder
development. However, Marx argues, that ultimately bourgeois
production will, in turn, start to hinder development too. Engels and
Marx saw the periodic commercial crises of capitalism as moments
when this economic system is put on trial. During these capitalist
crises, overproduction is followed by recession, greater exploitation,
and the development of new markets. As battles break out over wages,
the working day, and the intensity of work, the workers become
conscious of capitalist exploitation and act collectively against it.

In 1849, Marx published *Wage-Labor and Capital and Value, Price,
and Profit*. This work contains sketches of many of the basic economic
ideas that Marx would expand on in *Capital*. *Grundrisse,* an unfinished
book of 1857–8, also prepares for *Capital,* covering concepts such as
labor, production, and production relations. In 1859, Marx published
A Contribution to the Critique of Political Economy, a complex theoretical
treatment of money and commodities.* However, this did not feature
the concept of surplus value* which, in *Capital*, became Marx's unique
contribution to political economy.

Capital was the culmination of Marx's life work. He had planned
to write it over four volumes: the fourth volume to be a critique of

previous economic thinking. Marx created a draft version of this volume between 1862 and 1863, but it was not published until the twentieth century under the title *Theories of Surplus Value*.

Integration

Marx was both an intellectual and a revolutionary. In his early writings he speaks against the alienation* of man from his natural condition. In his later work the concept of alienation is absorbed into his description of the economic exploitation of the working class.* In the twentieth century this led to the idea that there was an early and a late Marx. This idea was especially prevalent among the Frankfurt School* of Marxists: a group of Marxist thinkers who were prominent in the 1960s. "Early Marx" focused on the need to overcome the alienated state of humanity. "Late Marx" focused on more mechanical economic solutions to social ills.

Marx's aim in writing *Capital* was to produce revolutionary change. He had developed a scientific analysis of the contradictions and exploitation at the heart of capitalism that *Capital* was intended to unmask. He amended the early chapters for the second edition in order to make the work more accessible, but the core ideas remained unchanged.

Nonetheless, there have been disputes about what Marx was saying in *Capital*. That debate has come about partly because the book was unfinished. Another factor is that Engels was responsible for editing volumes 2 and 3 and made additions and amendments of his own. Debate has arisen over the way Marx's words have been translated,[3] while Marxist economists disagree about the emphasis that should be placed on the different causes of crisis that Marx outlined.[4] Furthermore, the publication of every available document and letter that Marx wrote has opened up complex debates about the development of his entire thinking process. However, there is no indication that Marx himself sought to amend his fundamental framework or its conclusions during his lifetime.

Significance

In the twentieth century, *Capital* became the ideological inspiration and justification behind revolutionary socialist* and communist struggles to change the world. The book also gave birth to several schools of thought, all interested in assessing contemporary capitalist or post-capitalist societies.

The Russian Revolution* of 1917 established the first socialist government in Marx's name. Following the death of Vladimir Lenin,* the founder of the Soviet Union,* in 1924, the Soviet politician Joseph Stalin* rose to power. His version of socialism was Communist Party rule over a nationalized and bureaucratically planned economy.* Supporters of the Soviet politician Leon Trotsky* denounced the Stalinist system. They claimed that socialism required material prosperity and democratic control by the working class.

The dictatorial nature of the Soviet Union from the late 1920s onwards and, later, the formation of similar regimes in China* and Eastern Europe, led to a widespread belief within the advanced capitalist democracies that Marxism* automatically develops into a totalitarian dictatorship. There were, however, a number of occasion when communist states* tried to reform communism. The most dramatic attempts at reform occurred in the Hungarian Uprising* in 1956 and in Czechoslovakia* in 1968. When the European communist states collapsed* between 1989 and 1991 it was commonly presented as a rejection of Marx's theories. How accurate was that presentation? Marx is often seen to be significant because of what was done in his name. The perception of his importance has waxed and waned in line with the strength of the so-called socialist regimes. It is also possible to assess Marx on his own merit. A number of Marx-inspired schools of thought oppose the system of power established in Marx's name. Including communists,* Trotskyists,* and the Frankfurt School.

Since the global economic crisis* that began in 2007, Marx's reputation has grown. Interest in his critique of capitalism has been revived and sales of his works have increased. In addition, Marxism permeates academic life. It is hardly possible to discuss the family, or crime, or any other topic in the social sciences without encountering Marxist approaches to the subject. Curiously, the only exception to this is economics, where Marx's insights in *Capital* have been steadfastly ignored. Marx is one of the most important and controversial social thinkers of all time. His thoughts are likely to remain a permanent feature of academia.

NOTES

1   Karl Marx and Friedrich Engels, *Collected Works*, vol. 6 (London: Lawrence and Wishart, 1976), 487.

2   Marx and Engels, *Collected Works*, vol. 6, 498.

3   See Michael Heinrich, "Engels' Edition of the Third Volume of *Capital* and Marx's Original Manuscript," *Science and Society* 60, no. 4 (1996): 452–66.

4   See Andrew Kliman, *Reclaiming Marx's Capital: A Refutation of the Myth of Inconsistency* (Lanham, MD: Lexington Books, 2007).

SECTION 3
IMPACT

MODULE 9
THE FIRST RESPONSES

KEY POINTS

- The Marxist* labor theory of value* is an abstraction. It is difficult to relate it to real prices.

- Marx did not address this issue in detail. Friedrich Engels* argued the labor theory of value is a scientific approximation, rather than being absolutely precise.

- Marxists are split into two camps: revolutionaries and reformists.*

Criticism

The first response to Karl Marx's seminal work, *Capital: A Critique of Political Economy*, was muted. Sales of the book were poor and many of its readers found the ideas too difficult to understand. However, the German socialist parties* adopted Marx's ideas, which also found a ready audience in Russia despite the fact that capitalism* there was underdeveloped.

The first critiques of *Capital: A Critique of Political Economy* focused on Karl Marx's labor theory of value and the price paid for commodities.* The Austrian economist Eugen von Böhm-Bawerk* argued that Marx had not taken adequate account of how scarcity, supply and demand, and utility help to determine these values and prices.[1]

Marx argued that "the prices of production of all commodities produced in society—the totality of all branches of production—is equal to the sum of their values."[2] The Russian economist Ladislaus von Bortkiewicz* produced mathematical results in which total price did not equal total value, nor total profit equal total surplus value.* He argued that this disproved Marx's theory.[3]

❝ Capital withdraws from a sphere with a low rate of profit and wends its way to others that yield higher profit. This constant migration, the distribution of capital between the different spheres according to where the profit rate is rising and where it is falling, is what produces a relationship between supply and demand such that the average profit is the same in the various different spheres, and, values are therefore transformed into prices of production. ❞

Karl Marx, *Capital*

The German political theorist Eduard Bernstein* criticized Marx's concept of irreconcilable class antagonism and his emphasis on economic history. He described the labor theory of value as an entirely abstract, speculative hypothesis.[4] Bernstein's criticisms became the intellectual foundation of the reformist* trend in socialism. This argued that capitalism should be reformed, rather than overthrown.

The theory that it is labor that adds value to a commodity is fundamental to Marx's view of capitalism. If added (surplus) value is created in other ways then Marxian economics fails. This argument states that Marxian economics ignores the value added by entrepreneurialism.

Responses

Serious criticism of Marx's work did not begin until after his death, which meant Marx himself did not address the criticisms. After Marx's friend and collaborator Friedrich Engels* published the second volume of *Capital* in 1884 he initiated a "Prize Essay Competition". This was to encourage debate about the relationship between Marx's labor theory of value and real prices and profits. A discussion was published in the preface to volume 3.

Engels emphasized that scientific claims are not based on total precision, but are approximate. One key problem was the issue of how to translate Marx's theories about surplus value and average profit rates* into empirically verifiable data. This is still in question today. Is the labor theory of value purely theoretical or can it be verified with real data?

The Austrian-born economist Rudolf Hilferding* addressed Eugen von Böhm-Bawerk's argument that Marx had not paid sufficient attention to the impact of factors like scarcity, supply and demand, and utility on value. Hilferding claimed that Marx's theory concerned social relationships, whereas price reflects an individual's psychological relationship to a commodity (a thing is worth what someone is willing to pay for it, irrespective of how long the commodity takes to produce).[5] No real consensus over the issue of value was reached. As neoclassical economics* developed in the late nineteenth century, its adherents focused on the issue of supply and demand, and abandoned the labor theory of value altogether.

The Polish Marxist Rosa Luxemburg* criticized Bernstein. In her *Reform or Revolution* (1900) she claimed his ideas expressed the outlook and interests of individual capitalists who feared revolution and sought reform as a means to prevent it.

Conflict and Consensus

Debate about Marx's ideas helped shape twentieth-century world politics. In 1864 the First International* (also known as the International Working Men's Association) was created to promote global revolutionary change. Marx was the de facto leader but the organization was composed of diverse groups (e.g. British trade unionists, Italian nationalists, Russian anarchists). Each followed their own ideology and used different methods to fight for their goals.

In 1871, the First International supported Marx when he commented on the Paris Commune (a two-month-long revolt of

Parisians against the French government). During this revolt, the Commune established an egalitarian system of revolutionary democracy. Marx praised this, saying, "The working class* cannot simply lay hold on the ready-made state machinery and wield it for their own purpose." Marx saw the state as an instrument for class oppression. From the 1890s, socialists clashed over his concept of irreconcilable class antagonism, reformists argued for capitalism's reform, and revolutionaries argued for its overthrow.

Rosa Luxemburg defended a revolutionary interpretation of Marxism. The German political theorist Eduard Bernstein wanted reform, believing that Marx and Engels placed too much emphasis on economics as the force driving events. He said more emphasis should be put on the role of ideas, arguing that increasing monopolization of capital would diminish the severity of economic crises, and democracy would improve conditions for the working class.[6] Rosa Luxemburg disagreed, pointing out that capitalism was an international phenomenon, while states were only national concerns. This was another contradiction of the capitalist system. "Europe is only a link in the tangled chain of international connections and contradictions."[7] She believed that the global nature of capitalism would accelerate its decline.

The Russian revolutionary Vladimir Lenin* also believed that capitalism was entering its final era. He saw this stage as characterized by increasing monopolization. Lenin argued that large enterprises from powerful countries would push their nations into wars to redivide the world. In 1917, following the overthrow of the old Russian state during the Russian Revolution,* Lenin became the leader of the first state to be ruled by a Marxist party and ideology.

Marxist thought was still open to interpretation. The Russian economist Evgeni Preobrazhensky* proposed that scientific planning could replace Marx's law of value.* Forecasting and accounting, not market regulation, would gradually eliminate capitalist booms and slumps.[8] This idea was rejected. In the early 1930s, under the Soviet dictator Joseph Stalin,* most of the Russian economy was nationalized. Marx's emphasis on productive labor was used to determine the value of various types of labor (manual labor tended to be more highly paid than intellectual labor). Meanwhile, Trotskyists* cited Marx to claim that the economic and cultural prerequisites for socialism did not exist in Russia.

NOTES

1   Eugen von Böhm-Bawerk, *Karl Marx and the Close of his System* (Auburn, AL: Ludwig von Mises Institute, 1966).

2   Karl Marx, *Capital: A Critique of Political Economy*, vol. 3 (London: Penguin Books in association with New Left Review, 1992), 259.

3   Ladislaus von Bortkiewicz, *Value and Price in the Marxian System* (Chicoutimi: Bibliothèque Paul-Émile Boulet de l'Université du Québec à Chicoutimi, 2008).

4   See Eduard Bernstein, *Evolutionary Socialism: A Criticism and Affirmation* (New York: Schocken Books, 1909).

5   Rudolf Hilferding, *Boehm-Bawerk's Criticism of Marx* (Glasgow: Socialist Labour Press, 1919).

6   Bernstein, *Evolutionary Socialism,* 145.

7   Rosa Luxemburg in Richard Day, *Discovering Imperialism: Social Democracy to World War I* (Boston, MA: Brill, 2012), 454–5.

8   E. Preobrazhensky, *The New Economics* (Oxford: Clarendon Press, 1965).

MODULE 10
THE EVOLVING DEBATE

KEY POINTS

- Marx's ideas deeply influenced world history in the twentieth century.

- Two main issues divided Marxists: whether they supported revolution or reform; and their opinions about communist states.*

- The discussion about how economically backward countries could establish socialism* shaped much of world history after 1917.

Uses and Problems

The ideas expressed by Karl Marx in *Capital: A Critique of Political Economy* were applied in the "real world" following the Russian Revolution* of 1917.

Prior to the outbreak of World War I* in 1914, most members of the Second International*—an organization made up of socialists from across the world—supported the war. The Russian revolutionary, Vladimir Lenin,* opposed it. In his book, *Imperialism, the Highest Stage of Capitalism* (1916), he condemned the war as an imperialist affair that turned worker against worker, arguing that the war served the interests of the big banks and monopolies of the wealthiest countries. He led the Russian Revolution promising land, bread, and peace.

Once the revolutionaries had won, Marxists debated how to transform the backward Russian economy into a socialist one. They needed to secure agricultural resources for the cities but this caused conflict with the peasantry and resulted in the rise of a bureaucratic planned economy.* Under the Soviet dictator Joseph Stalin* a rigid

❝ The question of how a socialist society—which represents a totally new form of society—should be governed is one that world socialism was never able to answer satisfactorily in the past. Marx and Engels never actually encountered the comprehensive governance of a socialist country in practice, and most of their theorizations on the society of the future came in the form of predictions. **❞**

Xi Jinping, "Aligning Our Thinking with the Guiding Principles"

communist* ideology developed. This affected states across Eastern Europe and led to intellectual stagnation within socialism. Criticism of Stalin's regime was repressed in the Soviet Union and remained weak elsewhere.

The Great Depression* in the 1930s bolstered the influence of Marxism but during World War II* Fascist* victories in Europe destroyed most European Marxist groups. Following the Soviet Union's defeat of Germany in 1945, however, the Soviets occupied Central and Eastern Europe. Communists backed by the Soviet Union seized power in those states. Communist governments also came to power in countries outside Eastern Europe, such as China,* Cuba, Vietnam, Laos, and Cambodia.

By the late 1940s, tensions between the Soviet Union and the United States had evolved into the Cold War,* a conflict that dominated international relations from 1945 to 1991. It also affected economics. Until the 1970s, Keynesian* economic policy had been influential in Western European capitalism. This argued that the state should intervene to stimulate demand during economic crises.* But the right-wing governments of British Prime Minister Margaret Thatcher* and US President Ronald Reagan* favored neo-liberal* economic philosophy. They sought to roll back the state and destroy the influence of socialism. And in 1991, social unrest and rebellion in Eastern Europe brought down Europe's communist governments. The Soviet Union collapsed.* Marxism appeared to be a discredited ideology.

Schools of Thought

There are several schools of thought within Marxism. The most important are reformism,* Leninism,* Stalinism,* Trotskyism,* and market socialism.*

The German political theorist Eduard Bernstein* created reformism. He disputed Marx's labor theory of value* and opposed revolution. Instead, he advocated using democratic means to improve the condition of the working class.* Before the outbreak of World War I most socialist parties in the Second International*— an international socialist organization—supported his ideas. His thinking would influence the British Labour Party* and the German Social Democrats. However, the Polish Marxist Rosa Luxemburg* accused Bernstein of undermining Marxism.

The Russian revolutionary Vladimir Lenin* also opposed Bernstein. Lenin believed that imperialism* had unified the world, preparing the way for global socialism in which the working class would control the workers' state. Lenin argued that while the socialist revolution could begin in a backward country, to survive it would have to spread to developed countries.

Stalin also believed that socialism could be created in a backward country, because it established a system of bureaucratic state power. Under Stalin's communist rule, democratic debate was curtailed and opponents brutally repressed. Leon Trotsky* said Stalinism was not socialist, arguing that socialism has to be based on advanced production and culture, and that the state has to be administered by the working class. Trotsky wanted democracy in the Soviet Union, but with a planned economy.[1]

Market socialism emerged in the 1930s. The Austrian economist Friedrich von Hayek* argued that while free markets* respond flexibly to individual choices, using dynamic price fluctuations, planned economies can't react to these complex market signals.[2] The Polish economist Oskar Lange* disagreed. In *On the Economic Theory of Socialism* (1936) he stated that publicly owned enterprises could be just as responsive to changing demand as private ones.[3] His model showed how planners of state enterprises could adjust market prices in response to supply and demand.

In Current Scholarship

Marxism remains a major intellectual school of thought. The People's Republic of China is ruled by the Chinese Communist Party (CCP), over 80 million members strong. The CCP claims Marxism as its guiding ideology and describes China's social system as "socialism with Chinese characteristics."*[4] China has the world's largest population and its second largest economy. Its current leader Xi Jinping* says, "Officials cannot do without the guidance of Marxist philosophy."[5]

For the British academic David Harvey,* Marx's concept of primitive accumulation* is central to his relevance in the twenty-first century. Harvey is the most renowned Marxist economist today. He teaches a course on *Capital* at the City University of New York and argues that accumulation by dispossession is an important part of modern capitalism. Industries and their workforces may be relocated to undermine revolutionary threats. Production shifts from countries with high levels of union organization to countries where labor organizations are weak—"the bourgeoisie may evolve its own spatial strategies of dispersal, of divide and rule, of geographical disruptions to the rise of class forces that so clearly threaten its existence."[6] Harvey believes conflicts over the nature of urban life, rather than workplace conflicts, are the major focal point of the modern revolutionary struggle.

NOTES

1   Leon Trotsky, *The Revolution Betrayed: What is the Soviet Union, Where is it Going?* (New York: Pathfinder Press, 1991).

2   F. A. Hayek et al. *Collectivist Economic Planning: Critical Studies on the Possibilities of Socialism* (Auburn, AL: Ludwig von Mises Institute, 2009).

3   Oskar Lange, "On the Economic Theory of Socialism: Part One," *Review of Economic Studies* 4, no. 1 (1936): 53–71.

4   See Xie Chuntao, *Why and How the CPC Works in China* (Beijing: New World Press, 2011).

5   *People's Daily Online*, "Vice President Urges Officials to Enhance Study of Marxism," May 14, 2011, accessed October 1, 2013, http://english.people.com.cn/90001/90776/90785/7379801.html.

6   David Harvey, *Spaces of Hope* (Berkeley: University of California Press, 2000), 37.

MODULE 11
IMPACT AND INFLUENCE TODAY

KEY POINTS

- Marx's *Capital* has regained some influence in recent years. This is largely due to the global economic crisis* that began in 2007.

- The idea that capitalism* has inherent systemic flaws has gained support during recent years.

- Within mainstream economics the global economic crisis is viewed as a financial crisis. This has generated discussion on inequality and austerity rather than challenging the capitalist system.

Position

The role of Karl Marx's *Capital: A Critique of Political Economy* in current debate was deeply influenced by the collapse* of the socialist* model in the Soviet Union* and Eastern Europe. This discredited planned economics* and undermined communist* and socialist political authority. Marx's critique of capitalism appeared to be outdated because, for all its flaws, capitalism had outlived socialism.*

This was seen as a victory of free-market* philosophy over socialism. As a result, the ideological offensive against public ownership and state provision of welfare and services increased in many countries. A rise in private ownership popularized privatization. Even the reformist* model of socialism—comprehensive welfare provision within economies dominated by private-sector interests—came under pressure. This social model does, however, still exist in a few countries, particularly in Scandinavia

> ❝ Policy makers struggling to understand the barrage of financial panics, protests and other ills afflicting the world would do well to study the works of a long-dead economist: Karl Marx. The sooner they recognize we're facing a once-in-a-lifetime crisis of capitalism, the better equipped they will be to manage a way out of it. The spirit of Marx, who is buried in a cemetery close to where I live in north London, has risen from the grave amid the financial crisis and subsequent economic slump. The wily philosopher's analysis of capitalism had a lot of flaws, but today's global economy bears some uncanny resemblances to the conditions he foresaw. ❞
> George Magnus, "Give Karl Marx a Chance to Save the World Economy"

The global economic crisis that started in 2007 provoked an intellectual crisis within free-market, neoliberal* economic theory. This fueled a small revival of interest in Marxism and, although interest in *Capital* remains marginal, in Western academic debate the influence of Marxist* theories has increased. In the People's Republic of China,* where a rapprochement with free-market models took place in the early 2000s, a greater emphasis on Marxist-inspired explanations for crisis has been evident since 2008.[1]

In 2014, the French economist Thomas Piketty* published *Capital in the Twenty-First Century*. His book referenced Marx and led to a global debate on inequality. "Modern economic growth and the diffusion of knowledge have made it possible to avoid the Marxist apocalypse but have not modified the deep structures of capital and inequality—or in any case not as much as one might have imagined in the optimistic decades following [World War II*]."[2] Piketty argues that capitalism automatically produces extreme inequality and social tensions. These endanger democracy. He recommends that the state should intervene to counteract this.

Interaction

After the collapse of many communist states* in 1991, the American political scientist Francis Fukuyama* said that liberal democracy* had conquered the world and would be the final phase of human society.[3] He claims that the growth of the middle class undermined the appeal of Marxism. Although Fukuyama now fears that "the further development of technology and globalization undermines the middle class." They are being replaced by "hundreds of millions of new workers in developing countries."[4] This process can be seen as Marx's theory of proletarian internationalism.* Marx wrote, "The bourgeoisie* has stripped of its halo every occupation hitherto honored … It has converted the physician, the lawyer, the priest, the poet, the man of science, into its paid wage-laborers."[5]

Whether or not Marxist theory offers valid insights, in the Western world it remains at the margins of mainstream debate, tainted by its association with Stalinism.* Worldwide, however, Marxist thought remains active. In 1998 the socialist leader Hugo Chávez* became president of Venezuela. Advocating popular democratic control of resources and universal welfare and social provision, his government inspired political movements in Bolivia, Ecuador, Nicaragua, and Uruguay. But, since Chávez's death in 2013, Venezuela has suffered from a sharp economic crisis* that the socialist government has been unable to alleviate, despite possessing vast oil revenues.

The Chinese Communist Party spent over a decade considering the lessons of the collapse of the Soviet Union* and other European communist states. The conclusion drawn was that political power must remain exclusively in communist hands and ideological work must be improved.[6] Different perspectives on economic policy reflect an ongoing conflict between state and the private sector for dominance. One of the most influential economists is Justin Yifu Lin.* He proposes widespread privatization, free markets, and private ownership.[7] However, since 2008, the leadership of the Chinese Communist Party has re-emphasized their debt to Marxist theory. The expansion of the state sector, plus a major campaign against corruption, is seen as an attempt to reinforce the power of the party.

The Continuing Debate

The Polish philosopher Leszek Kołakowski* developed one of the most comprehensive critiques of Marx and Marxism.[8] He said Marx's concept of historical materialism* was groundbreaking and laid the basis for understanding history in a social context. Kolakowski sees Marx's description of economic factors as determining outcomes in "the last instance" as vague and unscientific. Kolakowski also disputed Marx's labor theory of value,* saying that while labor is an important component of value, the labor time and human skills in a commodity* cannot be precisely measured. Kolakowski regarded socialist states as "examples not of the abolition of exploitation but of exploitation in an extreme degree" where the "mass of society is excluded from decisions as to the use of means of production* and the distribution of income."[9] To limit such exploitation required democratic control and political freedom.

The Hungarian economist János Kornai* critiqued socialist political economy* in the twentieth century.[10] For Kornai, practical socialism reflects Marxist thought,[11] because public ownership and planning were "the two *basic* features of the economic order"[12] that Marx envisaged. Similarly, Marx was in line with Lenin* and Stalin's* views on democracy, seeing it solely as an instrument of class rule. While accepting that Marx offered new insight into society and praising his analysis of "states that differ from market equilibrium,"[13] Kornai rejects Marx's labor theory of value in favor of "theories of the real movements of prices, wages, costs, and profits."[14]

NOTES

1 See Cheng Enfu and Xin Xiangyang, "Fundamental Elements of the China Model," *International Critical Thought* 1, no. 1 (2011).

2 Thomas Piketty, *Capital in the Twenty-First Century*, trans. Arthur Goldhammer (Harvard, MA: Belknap Press, 2014), 1.

3 See Francis Fukuyama, *The End of History and the Last Man* (New York: Free Press, 2006).

4 Francis Fukuyama, "The Future of History," *Foreign Affairs* 91, no. 1 (2012).

5 Karl Marx and Friedrich Engels, *Collected Works*, vol. 6 (London: Lawrence and Wishart, 1976), 478.

6 David Shambaugh, *China's Communist Party: Atrophy and Adaptation* (Oakland: University of California Press, 2008).

7 Justin Yifu Lin, *Demystifying the Chinese Economy* (Cambridge: Cambridge University Press, 2012).

8 See Leszek Kołakowski, *Main Currents of Marxism: Its Origins, Growth and Dissolution* (Oxford: Oxford University Press, 1981), 1.

9 Kołakowski, *Main Currents of Marxism*, 334.

10 Janos Kornai, *The Socialist System: The Political Economy of Communism* (Oxford: Clarendon Press, 2007).

11 Janos Kornai, "Marx Through the Eyes of an East European Intellectual," *Social Research* 76, no. 3 (2009): 974.

12 Kornai, "Marx Through the Eyes," 975.

13 Kornai, "Marx Through the Eyes," 981.

14 Kornai, "Marx Through the Eyes," 972.

MODULE 12
WHERE NEXT?

KEY POINTS

- Political and economic exclusion create a fertile environment in which Marx's ideas can flourish.
- Marx's ideas will continue to influence proponents of state intervention, who seek to limit extreme inequality and maintain social stability.
- *Capital* has helped to shape how mankind views and organizes the world.

Potential

Interest in Karl Marx's masterpiece *Capital: A Critique of Political Economy* faded when Eastern Europe's communist states* fell. In 1992 the American political scientist Francis Fukuyama* published *The End of History and the Last Man*,[1] arguing that liberal democracy* is the ultimate social system. However, military conflict, including the War on Terror,* has undermined this vision, as have economic crisis* and growing economic disparity.

In 2008 the British journalist Francis Wheen* wrote, "Far from being buried under the rubble of the Berlin Wall,* Marx may only now be emerging in his true significance. He could yet become the most influential thinker of the twenty-first century."[2] And a 2014 report by the British Ministry of Defence predicts that economic, social, and political inequality "will continue to fuel perceptions of injustice among those whose expectations are not met. This will increase tension and instability, both within and between societies and result in expressions of unrest such as disorder, violence, criminality, terrorism and insurgency … Inequality may also lead to the resurgence

> ❝ The rediscovery of Marx in this period of capitalist crisis is because he predicted far more of the modern world than anyone else in 1848.* That is, I think, what has drawn the attention of a number of new observers to his work—paradoxically, first among business people and business commentators rather than the left. ❞

Eric Hobsbawm,* "A Conversation about Marx, Student Riots, the New Left, and the Milibands," *The Observer*

of not only anti-capitalist ideologies, possibly linked to religious, anarchist or nihilist movements, but also to populism and even Marxism."[3]

The Hungarian-born American business magnate George Soros* is one of the richest men on earth. Despite being famous for the impact of his speculative investments, Soros believes that free-market* ideology puts the existence of capitalism* and democracy in danger. "To put the matter simply, market forces, if they are given complete authority even in the purely economic and financial arenas, produce chaos and could ultimately lead to the downfall of the global capitalist system … The capitalist system by itself shows no tendency toward equilibrium. The owners of capital seek to maximize their profits. Left to their own devices, they would continue to accumulate capital until the situation became unbalanced."[4]

If capitalism is able to satisfy material wants and to contain discontent within its democratic framework, socialism* will probably remain of marginal interest. However, economic and political exclusion may see Marx's ideas flourishing again. Within academia, Marx's combination of scientific analysis and moral outrage, his unveiling of hidden forms of exploitation, and his exposure of the material motives that lie behind everyday language and behavior, ensures that *Capital* will remain an influential text within the social sciences.

Future Directions

In the twentieth century the influence of Marx's ideas was closely intertwined with world politics. Wherever Marxism became a state ideology it became taboo to question the way it was interpreted. But fields other than politics were also influenced by Marx. The Marxist German playwright Bertolt Brecht* wrote plays with a political and social message that aimed to make audiences think.[5] The Soviet film director Sergei Eisenstein* used montage to produce images of revolutionary experience. The Austrian psychoanalyst Wilhelm Reich* combined Marxist ideas with Sigmund Freud's* sexual theory to argue that political revolution needed to be preceded by sexual revolution.[6] The Frankfurt School,* a group of Marxists active in the 1960s, gave rise to critical studies of language and culture.

In today's world the most influential Marxist is China's* leader Xi Jinping.* Outside China few people read his speeches, but his ideas shape his country's fate. Jinping emphasizes that Marxism is China's guiding ideology. This position, along with a radical campaign against corruption, is designed to strengthen support for the Chinese Communist Party and appease social discontent. Although many Western Marxists believe that China is now a capitalist country, Jinping's emphasis on the central role of public ownership and his outright opposition to parliamentary democracy indicate that China will remain a communist state for the foreseeable future.

Far-left movements—Syriza* and Podemos*—have recently made headway in Greece and Spain respectively. Within these parties there are politicians who are in favor of different versions of Marxism to oppose the European Union's current focus on economic austerity.

Summary

The fall of the Berlin Wall in 1989 was followed by a period of growth and stability in most of the world's wealthy countries. As capitalism and democracy spread to many former communist countries, Marx's analysis of capitalism seemed irrelevant. But the global economic crisis* of 2007–9 revealed structural and systemic flaws in capitalism that revived interest in Marx's ideas.

Marx wrote as an "outsider." In doing so, he offered the reader a wide range of unexpected ways of looking at apparently mundane things. *Capital* is a genuinely multidisciplinary work. Scholars, writers, and artists have adopted its ideas. The book not only investigates the nature of the society around us, but explores how human behavior, morality, and culture are formed, and challenges many apparently common-sense opinions about life. As a historical document it provides the reader with penetrating insight into a revolutionary ideology that brought about sweeping changes to society. Its enduring influence lies in the way *Capital* exposes exploitative human relations and motivates people to change them. The British academic David Harvey says it shows the reader, "that there is an immense array of resources out there that can shed light on the way we live the life we do."[7]

NOTES

1   Francis Fukuyama, *The End of History and the Last Man* (New York: Free Press, 2006).

2   Francis Wheen, *Marx's Das Kapital: A Biography* (New York: Grove Press, 2008), 120.

3   UK Ministry of Defence, *Global Strategic Trends: Out to 2045,* April 30, 2014, accessed March 20, 2015, https://www.gov.uk/government/uploads/ system/uploads/attachment_data/file/328036/DCDC_GST_5_Secured.pdf, 22.

4   George Soros, *The Crisis of Global Capitalism: Open Society Endangered* (New York: PublicAffairs, 1998), xxvi.

5   Bertolt Brecht, *The Messingkauf Dialogues* (London: Methuen, 1965).

6   Wilhelm Reich, *The Mass Psychology of Fascism* (New York: Farrar, Straus and Giroux, 1970).

GLOSSARY

GLOSSARY OF TERMS

1848: a year in which revolutions erupted throughout Europe, demanding the end of autocracy, democratic rights, and national unity or national independence. They were defeated in 1849.

Abstract labor: the expenditure of time when working, regardless of the nature of the product. This produces exchange value.

Alienation: Marx's early work discusses the concept of man being alienated from his natural condition, or "species-being," by a lack of control and ownership over labor and the labor process. See Karl Marx, *Economic and Philosophic Manuscripts of 1844.*

Anti-colonialism: a political science and international relations concept used to explain any form of opposition to imperialism, colonialism, and empire.

Berlin Wall: a fortified barrier that stood from 1961 to 1989, encircling the Western section of Berlin. It was used to prevent East Germans from leaving their country and became a symbol of the conflict between social systems. The fall of the Berlin Wall is commonly regarded as the beginning of the end of communism.

Bourgeoisie: Marx uses this term as another way to refer to the capitalists, although he also uses it more broadly to refer to wealthy classes in general.

Capitalism: this is a term Marx did not use, but is generally used to refer to a society dominated by the capitalist mode of production.

Capitalist: one who believes in an economic and political system in which a country's trade and industry are controlled by private businesses for profit, rather than by the state.

Capitalist class: those who live from the wealth created by workers engaged in commodity production.

Capitalist mode of production: according to Marx, the capitalist mode of production is characterized as generalized commodity production organized for profit. Private owners of the means of production (the land, inputs, and machinery) extract surplus value from the workers and society is organized in the image of these capitalist productive relations under the dominance of the capitalist class.

China: the Chinese Communist Party established the People's Republic of China in 1949 after a long civil war. Its government claims to be inspired by the ideas of Karl Marx.

Class struggle: the conflict between classes. Under capitalism, Marx says the main class struggle is between the workers and the capitalists.

Cold War: the period between 1945 and 1989, characterized by tense relations between the Soviet Union and the United States and their respective allies.

Collapse of the Soviet Union: refers to the dissolution of the Soviet Union into different nations in 1991. This "collapse" is commonly regarded as the final defeat of communism.

Commodity: Marx argues that commodities are things that satisfy human wants and needs, material or immaterial, and they simultaneously possess use value and exchange value.

Communism: Marx presents two phases of communist society, the lower and the higher. In the lower stage (often called socialism) the new society has features left over from capitalism, including the money relations of wage labor and inequality. Administration is based on democratic control by the working class. Public property is dominant. In the higher phase of communism, everyone works as they choose to, money disappears and administration requires no compulsion.

Communist: one who advocates the common control of the means of the production and the management of the economy.

Communist League: founded in 1847, the League was a predominantly German, international revolutionary organization, in which Marx and Engels were leading figures.

Communist Manifesto: a pamphlet written by Marx and Engels, first published in 1848. It sets the struggle for communism in a historical context and explains the revolutionary doctrines of Marx and Engels in popular form.

Communist parties: parties that advocate communism. They may differ in their views about communist states.

Communist states: also known in academia as communist party-states. These are societies where a communist party dominates the state (although it may not be called the "Communist Party"). They generally have planned economies.

Constant capital: the value of goods and materials required to produce a commodity. This contrasts with variable capital, which is the wages paid for the production of a commodity.

Czechoslovakia 1968: a Communist government in Czechoslovakia supported democratic rights and popular control of the economy and society. Soviet troops invaded in August 1968 and defeated the movement.

Dead labor: this is labor carried out in the past and crystallized into instruments of production, raw materials, and so on. Marx argues that it does not produce any new value.

Dialectical materialism: this encapsulates the two philosophical roots of Marxism. According to this doctrine, social change is driven by struggle between contradictory social classes over the material means of production.

Dialectics: a philosophy that proposes that change and progress are driven by inner contradictions.

Economic crisis: Marx's *Capital* examines various ways that capitalism enters crises. Economic crisis generally involves an economic contraction that reduces economic activity and results in many workers becoming poorer or losing their jobs.

Enlightenment: an era of intellectual awakening in philosophy and the sciences in the seventeenth and eighteenth centuries.

Exchange value: the amount of money or other commodities that something can be exchange for.

Fascism: a political movement mainly based on the middle class and the poorest sections of society that aims to smash workers' organizations and to impose the dictatorship of a single leader. It promotes nationalism, protects capitalist property relations, and abolishes independent workers' organizations.

Feudalism: a system of political and economic power based on obligations. In England, the monarchy granted land-holding to lords to whom peasants were bonded.

First International (1864–1876): also known as the International Working Men's Association; an organization set up to promote revolutionary change across the world. Karl Marx was its de facto leader.

Frankfurt School: a group of Marxist intellectuals who became influential in the 1960s. They included Herbert Marcuse (1898–1979), Jürgen Habermas (b. 1929) and Theodor W. Adorno (1903–69).

Free market: an economic system in which supply and demand are unregulated or minimally regulated.

French Revolution: a period of deep political and social transformation in France that took place between 1789 and 1799. It influenced the course of Western history as a whole.

German socialist parties: the various socialist parties and organizations that merged to become the German Social Democratic Party in 1875.

Global Economic Crisis of 2007–9: also known as the Great Recession, a period when production, wages, and living standards in most advanced capitalist countries fell and remained below their peak for a number of years.

Great Depression: a sharp economic contraction and a prolonged crisis that began in 1929. It led to mass unemployment and political polarization in Europe and the US. As a result, a fascist party (the Nazi

Party) led by Adolf Hitler came to power in Germany in 1933. This led to World War II.

Historical materialism: the application of the study of history using economic and social production as the central reference points.

Hungarian Uprising: an uprising in 1956 against the Hungarian Communist state that opposed Soviet occupation and advocated democratic communism/socialism instead. It was suppressed by force.

Imperialism: a method of economic and political exploitation of poor countries by rich countries. It often involves military conflict, conquest, and bullying, as well as economic manipulation and exploitation.

Industrialization: economic development based on factory production, a division of labor, and urbanization.

Industrial Revolution: A period of rapid industrial development between about 1760 and 1840. New machines and power sources were applied in manufacturing industry.

Input–output analysis: the analysis of how a change in one part of a system affects its other parts.

Keynesian: this refers to state intervention to stimulate demand in economic crises, based on the thinking of British economist John Maynard Keynes (1883–1946). It is also associated with the comprehensive welfare provision in some European countries from 1945 to 1975.

Labor movement: the organized working class, also known as the workers' movement.

Labor power: the worker's ability to work, which is what is sold to the capitalist for wages. Owners then seek to make profits by selling the products produced by workers.

Labor theory of value: the value of a good or service that is determined by the total labor time required to produce it.

Labour Party: a British political party founded by trade unions in 1900. It advocated socialism but never adopted Marxism as its philosophy. It became a party that seeks reforms within capitalism.

Law of motion: a series of relationships that shape the way an economic system functions.

Law of the Tendential Fall in the Rate of Profit (LTFRP theory): a law of political economy put forth by Karl Marx that states that the rate of profit has a tendency to fall with the progress of capitalist production.

Law of value: the Marxist concept of the law of value refers to the automatic functioning of the capitalist economy driven by the search for profits in competitive markets.

Leninism: the theory and practice of communism developed by Vladimir Lenin. It deals with the importance of political leadership and a proletarian revolution.

Liberal democracy: a political system that emphasizes human and civil rights, regular and free elections between competing political parties, and adherence to the rule of law.

Living labor: human work to make things.

Market socialism: theory and practice using market incentives and mechanisms in an economy dominated by public ownership.

Marxism: refers to the ideas developed by Marx and Engels, particularly dialectical materialism, historical materialism, and scientific socialism.

Materialism: a philosophical trend which sees the material world as the foundation and determinant of thinking.

Means of production: the material inputs used in production. This does not include living labor.

Mode of production: this combines the productive forces of a society and the relations between people in the productive process.

Neoclassical economics: this looks at how scarce resources are allocated in markets and how the behavior of consumers and producers affects their assumed impulses and patterns of action derived therefrom. Neoclassical economics focuses on prices, outputs, and income distribution in markets governed by supply and demand.

Neoliberalism: generally seen as political and economic theory that supports free trade, privatization, minimal government intervention in business, and cuts in public expenditure on social services and welfare provision.

Planned economy: an economy in which the government determines prices, wages, production, and investment.

Podemos: a left-wing political party in Spain founded in 2014.

Political economy: this is the study of the combination of economics, law, and politics, and the examination of institutions in different social and economic systems. Theorists of this classical school of economics shared a belief that free markets self-regulate economic activities. Its main thinkers were Adam Smith (1723–90), Thomas Malthus (1766–1834), Jean-Baptiste Say (1767–1832), David Ricardo (1772–1823), and John Stuart Mill (1806–73).

Primitive accumulation: described by Marx as a process of violent acquisition of wealth at the birth of capitalism. It is not based on equal exchange.

Proletarian internationalism: Marx's theory of proletarian internationalism means that workers of different countries have more in common than workers and employers of the same country. In other words, Marx believed that workers everywhere should unite against a common enemy: capitalism.

Prussia: a German state mostly located in north-eastern Europe. It played the leading role in the unification of Germany in 1871 and was dissolved in 1947.

Reformism: a political trend in the socialist movement that advocates reform within capitalism as an alternative to a revolution to overthrow capitalism.

Revolutionaries and reformists: Vladimir Lenin (1870–1924), Rosa Luxemburg (1871–1919), and Leon Trotsky (1879–1940) are three of Marx's revolutionary followers, whereas Eduard Bernstein (1850–1932), Karl Kautsky (1854–1938), and Jean Jaurès (1859–1914) are reformists.

Russian Revolution: this revolution happened in two stages: the revolt of February 1917 that saw the overthrow of the Romanov monarchy, and the revolt of October 1917 that brought the Bolsheviks to power and brought a Marxist party to power for the first time. Its leaders sought to create a socialist society and were inspired by the ideas of Karl Marx.

Scientific socialism: the concept intended to contrast with visions of socialism based on ideal intellectual constructs, which Marx and Engels called utopian socialism. Scientific socialism would be based on an accurate assessment of the world as it is. The socialism it creates will come out of existing material conditions. This is why *Capital* contains so little reference to the future socialist society.

Second International (1889–1916): an organization, also known as the Socialist International, made up of various socialist parties. The International grew rapidly in Europe but in 1914 most national sections voted to support World War I. This resulted in the collapse of the organization in 1916. A loosely connected Socialist International replaced it and still exists today.

Socialism: this encompasses a wide range of theories and political movements. Socialists believe that various forms of public ownership will enable human needs and the promotion of egalitarian opportunities and outcomes to be prioritized.

"Socialism with Chinese Characteristics": the official definition used in China to denote its economic and political system since the 1980s.

Socialist: one who believes in the collective ownership of the means of production and the collective management of the economy.

Socialist society: Marx envisages that a socialist society will be organized on the basis of common ownership and democratic administration. He uses the term socialism interchangeably with the term communism but he expects there to be a lower and higher phase of communism.

Soviet Union: a country that existed from 1922 to 1991. It was initially established as a union of socialist republics surrounding Russia but it was hoped all countries in the world would also turn socialist and join the union. It became a union dominated by Russia.

Stalinism: this refers to the policies, practices, and ideologies of communist parties that supported bureaucratic dictatorships (such as that of Joseph Stalin) in the USSR and Eastern Europe. It is often used to refer to ruling communist parties and sometimes to authoritarian or undemocratic political practices in general. Leon Trotsky was the most prominent theorist to develop a theory of Stalinism, which he called a degenerated workers' state.

Surplus value: Marx claims that the value of commodities is equal to the average socially necessary labor time required to make them. Surplus value is the difference between the value of labor power and the value it adds to the products under capitalism.

Syriza: a coalition of far-left political parties elected to government in Greece in January 2015.

Third International (1919–1943): an organization inspired by the Russian Revolution, also known as the Communist International or Comintern. It promoted international revolution but increasingly became an instrument of Soviet foreign policy. Stalin dissolved it after Britain and the US agreed to Soviet dominance of Central and Eastern Europe after 1945.

Trotskyism: the political and economic principles developed by Leon Trotsky (1879–1940), especially the belief that socialism should be established throughout the world by continuing revolution.

Trotskyists: followers of Leon Trotsky who split into many different groups around the world. They never became a significant political force.

Use value: how much one benefits from an item. This contrasts with exchange value or how much one can sell that item for.

Utopian socialism: a term used by Marx and Engels to describe imaginary socialist societies or experimental communities not based on material reality. It refers to visions of ideal societies based on egalitarian principles.

War on Terror: a term often applied to the American-led military campaign against terrorist groups involved in the September 11, 2001 terrorist attacks on the United States. It combines increased mechanisms for global surveillance with low-to-high intensity military conflicts around the world.

Workers' movement: the organized expression of working-class struggles to improve their conditions and bring about social change; sometimes called the labor movement.

Working class: those who live by selling their labor power for a wage

World War I: a war that took place from 1914 to 1918 between the world's most powerful nations. Popular uprisings and revolts ended the war—in Russia in 1917, and in Germany in 1918.

World War I: an international conflict between 1914 and 1918 centered in Europe and involving the major economic world powers of the day.

World War II: a war that took place from 1939 to 1945 involving the world's most powerful nations. The ruling dictatorships in Japan, Germany, and Italy were defeated by an alliance led by Russia, the US, and Britain.

PEOPLE MENTIONED IN THE TEXT

Eduard Bernstein (1850–1932) was a German Social Democratic politician. He believed that evolutionary change within capitalism would gradually bring about socialism. He wrote *The Preconditions of Socialism* in 1899.

Eugen von Böhm-Bawerk (1851–1914) was an Austrian economist and government finance minister. He wrote a critique of Marx's labor theory of value that argues that Marx's abstract theory of value does not match Marx's theory of prices.

Ladislaus von Bortkiewicz (1868–1931) was a Russian economist who taught at Berlin University. Bortkiewicz pointed to flaws in Marx's method of transforming value into prices.

Bertolt Brecht (1898–1956) was a German playwright inspired by Marxist ideas. His theatre attempted to develop a method of performance that made people question the way society is organized.

Hugo Chávez (1954–2013) was the president of Venezuela from 1998 until 2013. He advocated democratic change to enhance the economic and political position of the poor. In the 10 years before he died he became a radical socialist and founded the United Socialist Party of Venezuela.

Sergei Eisenstein (1898–1948) was a Soviet filmmaker. He dealt with social issues and presented class struggle and revolution in his cinematic montage.

Friedrich Engels (1820–95) was a German revolutionary philosopher and Marx's closest collaborator. Engels popularized Marx's ideas and the socialist movement after Marx's death.

Ludwig Feuerbach (1804–72) was a German philosopher who studied under Hegel and developed materialist philosophy. His book *The Essence of Christianity* (1841) presented God as a reflection of humanity.

Charles Fourier (1772–1837) was a French philosopher and early socialist. He criticized the failure of the French Revolution to live up to its ideals and believed that the environment influences behavior. He proposed cooperative forms of society based on human passions as an alternative model. His *Theory of the Four Movements* was first published in French anonymously in 1808.

Sigmund Freud (1856–1939) was a Austrian neurologist and founder of psychoanalysis. He investigated the role of the unconscious in mental health and viewed the repression of childhood sexual experiences as being central to the formation of a person's mental outlook and character.

Francis Fukuyama (b. 1952) is an American political scientist who worked for the RAND corporation and currently for Stanford University. His most famous book is the *End of History and the Last Man* (1992); it argues that liberal democracy is the end point in the progress of human social systems.

Andrew Glyn (1943–2007) was a British economist who taught at Oxford University. He co-wrote *British Capitalism, Workers and the Profits Squeeze* (1972) with Robert Sutcliffe. He argued that falling profits were caused by improvements to workers' wages.

Henryk Grossman (1881–1950) was a Polish economist who worked in academia in Germany. He developed a Marxist model of the economic breakdown of capitalism.

David Harvey (b. 1935) is a British-born Marxist geographer who teaches at the City University of New York. He writes on the social geography of urban life and teaches a course on Marx's *Capital*.

Friedrich von Hayek (1899–1992) was an Austrian economist who taught at the London School of Economics, Chicago University, and Freiburg University. He inspired an economic philosophy known as neoliberalism, which was adopted by conservative governments in the UK and US in the 1980s.

Georg Wilhelm Friedrich Hegel (1770–1831) was a German philosopher who revived dialectical thought and applied it to historical and intellectual development. Dialectical philosophy considers change and progress to be driven by inner contradictions.

Rudolf Hilferding (1877–1941) was an Austrian Marxist economist and leading theorist of German social democracy. He developed a theory of imperialism based on Marx's ideas.

Adolf Hitler (1889–1945) was the founder of the National Socialist (Nazi) Party and dictator of Nazi Germany from 1933 to 1945. He claimed that Germans were racially superior and sought to annihilate the Jews and destroy the influence of Marxism.

Eric Hobsbawm (1917–2012) was a British Marxist historian who taught in London and Cambridge. He wrote extensively on modern history.

John Maynard Keynes (1883–1946) was a British economist, civil servant, and government advisor-supporter of the capitalist economic system. He believed that capitalism suffers periodic crises but government intervention can minimize the impact.

Andrew Kliman (b. 1955) is an American Marxist who teaches at Pace University. His work on Marx's theory of the tendency for the rate of profit to fall relates to contemporary crisis theory.

János Kornai (b. 1928) is a Hungarian economist and perhaps the foremost theoretician on the characteristics of the socialist system. He believes that the Marxist ideology of ruling communist parties is the primary factor that generated the dictatorial nature of the socialist systems around the world.

Leszek Kołakowski (1927–2009) was a Polish philosopher and historian. His three-volume *Main Currents in Marxism* (1976) is a highly acclaimed criticism of Marxist thought. Kołakowski concludes that Stalinism was the inevitable outcome of the doctrines of Marxism.

Oskar Lange (1904–65) was a Polish economist and participant in the Market Socialism debate with von Mises and Hayek in the 1930s. He developed a theoretical model of market socialism in which prices were adjusted to market signals by the planning organizations of publicly owned enterprises.

Vladimir Lenin (1870–1924) was a Russian revolutionary and anti-imperialist who led the Bolsheviks in the October 1917 Revolution, and became the leader of the first state to be ruled by a Marxist party and ideology. He developed organizational tactics based on centralized discipline and democratic discussion, and studied the nature of revolutions in an imperialist era.

Wassily Leontief (1906–99) was a Russian-born economist who developed models of economic sectors and their relations. These were applied to computer modeling of the United States economy.

Justin Yifu Lin (b. 1952) is professor and honorary dean of the National School of Development at Peking University in China. He is the former chief economist and senior vice-president of the World Bank.

Rosa Luxemburg (1871–1919) was a Polish Marxist also active on the left wing of German social democracy. She was imprisoned for opposing World War I, helped found the German Communist Party in 1918, and was murdered in 1919.

Ludwig von Mises (1881–1973) was an Austrian economist who argued that a socialist state is unable to organize an efficient and complex economy due to the complexity of economic calculations that is required.

Robert Owen (1771–1858) was a Welsh manufacturer, philanthropist, and socialist. He created model enterprises and established collectivist communities in Britain and the United States, and founded the British cooperative movement.

Thomas Piketty (b. 1971) is a French economist and a professor of economics at the London School of Economics. His work *Capital in the Twenty-First Century* (2014) is widely respected and studies inequality over the last 250 years.

Evgeni Preobrazhensky (1886–1937) was a Russian revolutionary and economist. He developed a theory of transformation to socialism by means of exploiting pre-socialist economic forms to acquire socialist capital.

Ronald Reagan (1911–2004) was president of the United States from 1981 to 1989. He took an aggressive anti-communist stance internationally, sharply increased US military spending, and promoted free markets and anti-trade unionism.

Wilhelm Reich (1897–1957) was an Austrian psychoanalyst who tried to integrate sexual liberation with Marxist revolutionary ideas. He abandoned Marxism and became interested in the search for energy fields. He died in prison in the United States.

David Ricardo (1772–1823) was a British political economist. He advocated global free trade and a belief in mutual benefit through specialization.

Michael Roberts (b. 1946) is a British Marxist economist. He works primarily on questions related to the Marxist theory of crisis.

Henri de Saint-Simon (1760–1825)—in full, Claude Henri de Rouvroy, Comte de Saint-Simon—was a French philosopher who believed society should be more rationally and collectively organized based on scientific principles, planning, and expert administration.

Adam Smith (1723–90) was a Scottish economist and philosopher. He was a pioneer in the study of political economy.

George Soros (b. 1930) is an influential Hungarian-born businessman who also promotes various political and philanthropic projects.

Joseph Stalin (1878–1953) was a Georgian revolutionary who became the leader of the Soviet Union from 1924 until 1953. The dictatorial rule he established is sometimes called Stalinism. He argued that socialism did not require advanced productive forces or the overthrow of capitalism elsewhere.

Margaret Thatcher (1925–2013) was British prime minister from 1979 to 1990. She promoted privatization, anti-communism, and anti-trade unionism.

Leon Trotsky (1879–1940) was a Russian revolutionary leader during the first years of existence of the USSR. In the 1930s he believed that a bureaucratic caste usurped control over the planned economy in the Soviet Union. He was expelled from the Communist Party, exiled from the Soviet Union and finally assassinated in Mexico.

Jenny von Westphalen (1814–81) was a German who married Karl Marx in 1843. Her father was Baron Ludwig von Westphalen.

Baron Ludwig von Westphalen (1770–1842) was a German-Prussian aristocrat and government official. A mentor of the young Karl Marx.

Francis Wheen (b. 1957) is a British journalist and writer. He is the author of *Karl Marx* (1999) and of *Marx's Das Kapital: A Biography* (2006).

Xi Jinping (b. 1953) is the General Secretary of the Communist Party of China and the Chinese head of state.

WORKS CITED

WORKS CITED

Bernstein, Eduard. *Evolutionary Socialism: A Criticism and Affirmation*. New York: Schocken Books, 1961.

Böhm-Bawerk, Eugen von and Rudolf Hilferding. *Karl Marx and the Close of His System*. Auburn, AL: Ludwig von Mises Institute, 1966.

Bortkiewicz, Ladislaus von. *Value and Price in the Marxian System*. Chicoutimi: Bibliothèque Paul-Émile Boulet de l'Université du Québec à Chicoutimi, 2008.

Brecht, Bertolt. *The Messingkauf Dialogues*. London: Methuen, 1965.

Chuntao, Xie. *Why and How the CPC Works in China*. Beijing: New World Press, 2011.

Day, Richard. *Discovering Imperialism: Social Democracy to World War I*. Boston, MA: Brill, 2012.

Enfu, Cheng, and Xin Xiangyang. "Fundamental Elements of the China Model." *International Critical Thought* 1, no. 1 (2011): 2–10.

Fourier, Charles, Ian Patterson, and Gareth Stedman Jones. *The Theory of the Four Movements*. Translated by Ian Patterson. New York: Cambridge University Press, 1996.

Fukuyama, Francis. *The End of History and the Last Man*. New York: Free Press, 2006.

"The Future of History: Can Liberal Democracy Survive the Decline of the Middle Class?" *Foreign Affairs*, 91, no. 1 (2012).

Glyn, Andrew and Robert Sutcliffe. *British Capitalism, Workers and the Profits Squeeze*. Harmondsworth: Penguin, 1972.

Harvey, David. *Spaces of Hope*. Berkeley: University of California Press, 2000.

A Companion to Marx's Capital. London and New York: Verso, 2010.

The Enigma of Capital: And the Crises of Capitalism. London: Profile Books, 2010.

Hayek, F. A., N. G. Pierson, L. von Mises, and E. Barone. *Collectivist Economic Planning: Critical Studies on the Possibilities of Socialism*. Auburn, AL: Ludwig von Mises Institute, 2009.

Heinrich, Michael. "Engels' Edition of the Third Volume of *Capital* and Marx's Original Manuscript." *Science and Society* 60, no. 4 (1996): 452–66.

Hilferding, Rudolf. *Boehm-Bawerk's Criticism of Marx*. Glasgow: Socialist Labour Press, 1919.

Kliman, Andrew. *Reclaiming Marx's Capital: A Refutation of the Myth of Inconsistency*. Lanham, MD: Lexington Books, 2007.

The Failure of Capitalist Production: Underlying Causes of the Great Recession. London: Pluto Press, 2012.

Kołakowski, Leszek. *Main Currents of Marxism: Its Origins, Growth and Dissolution*. Oxford: Oxford University Press, 1981.

Kornai, Janos. *The Socialist System: The Political Economy of Communism*. Oxford: Clarendon Press, 2007.

"Marx through the Eyes of an East European Intellectual." *Social Research* 76, no. 3 (2009): 965–86.

Lange, Oskar. "On the Economic Theory of Socialism: Part One." *Review of Economic Studies* 4, no. 1 (1936): 53–71.

Lenin, V. I. *Imperialism: The Highest Stage of Capitalism*. Sydney: Resistance, 1999.

Lin, Justin Yifu. *Demystifying the Chinese Economy*. Cambridge: Cambridge University Press, 2012.

Luxemburg, Rosa. *Reform or Revolution*. Mineola, NY: Dover Publications, 2006.

People's Daily Online, "Vice President Urges Officials to Enhance Study of Marxism." May 14, 2011. Accessed October 1, 2013. http://english.people.com.cn/90001/90776/90785/7379801.html.

Marx, Karl. *A Contribution to the Critique of Political Economy*. Moscow: Progress Publishers, 1970.

Wage-Labor and Capital and Value, Price, and Profit. New York: International Publishers, 1976.

Theories of Surplus-Value. Moscow: Progress, 1990.

Capital: A Critique of Political Economy. Vol. 1. London: Penguin Books in association with New Left Review, 1992.

Capital: A Critique of Political Economy. Vol. 2. London: Penguin Books in association with New Left Review, 1992.

Capital: A Critique of Political Economy. Vol. 3. London: Penguin Books in association with New Left Review, 1992.

Grundrisse: Foundations of the Critique of Political Economy (Rough Draft). London and New York: Penguin Books in association with New Left Review, 1993.

Economic and Philosophic Manuscripts of 1844. London: Martino Fine Books, 2011.

Marx, Karl, and Friedrich Engels. *Collected Works. Vol. 5*. London: Lawrence and Wishart, 1976.

Collected Works. Vol. 6. London: Lawrence and Wishart, 1976.

Collected Works. Vol. 20. London: Lawrence and Wishart, 1985

Collected Works. Vol. 22. London: Lawrence and Wishart, 1986.

Collected Works. Vol. 42. London: Lawrence and Wishart, 1987.

Collected Works. Vol. 24. London: Lawrence and Wishart, 1989.

Collected Works. Vol. 33. London: Lawrence and Wishart, 1991.

The Communist Manifesto. London and New York: Penguin Books, 2002.

Medema, Steven G., and Warren J. Samuels. *The History of Economic Thought: A Reader*. New York: Psychology Press, 2003.

Needham, Joseph, Kenneth Girdwood Robinson, Ray Huang, and Mark Elvin. *Science and Civilisation in China*. Vol. 7, Part 2. Cambridge: Cambridge University Press, 2004.

Piketty, Thomas. *Capital in the Twenty-First Century*. Translated by Arthur Goldhammer. New York: Belknap Press, 2014.

Pradella, Lucia. "Imperialism and Capitalist Development in Marx's *Capital.*" *Historical Materialism* 21, no.2 (2013): 117–47.

Preobrazhensky, E. *The New Economics*. Oxford: Clarendon Press, 1965.

Reich, Wilhelm. *The Mass Psychology of Fascism*. New York: Farrar, Straus and Giroux, 1970.

Roberts, Michael. *The Great Recession.* London: Lulu, 2009.

Shambaugh, David. *China's Communist Party: Atrophy and Adaptation*. Oakland: University of California Press, 2008.

Smith, A., and B. Mazlish. *The Wealth of Nations: Representative Selections*. Mineola, NY: Dover, 1961.

Soros, George. *The Crisis of Global Capitalism: Open Society Endangered*. New York: PublicAffairs, 1998.

Trotsky, Leon. *Permanent Revolution Results and Prospects.* New York: Merit, 1969.

The Revolution Betrayed: What Is the Soviet Union, Where Is It Going? New York: Pathfinder Press, 1991.

UK Ministry of Defence. *Global Strategic Trends: Out to 2045,* April 30, 2014. Accessed March 20, 2015. https://www.gov.uk/government/uploads/system/uploads/attachment_data/file/328036/DCDC_GST_5_Secured.pdf.

Wheen, Francis. *Karl Marx: A Life*. New York: W. W. Norton, 2001.

Marx's Das Kapital: A Biography. New York: Grove Press, 2008.

THE MACAT LIBRARY
BY DISCIPLINE

AFRICANA STUDIES

Chinua Achebe's *An Image of Africa: Racism in Conrad's Heart of Darkness*
W. E. B. Du Bois's *The Souls of Black Folk*
Zora Neale Huston's *Characteristics of Negro Expression*
Martin Luther King Jr's *Why We Can't Wait*
Toni Morrison's *Playing in the Dark: Whiteness in the American Literary Imagination*

ANTHROPOLOGY

Arjun Appadurai's *Modernity at Large: Cultural Dimensions of Globalisation*
Philippe Ariès's *Centuries of Childhood*
Franz Boas's *Race, Language and Culture*
Kim Chan & Renée Mauborgne's *Blue Ocean Strategy*
Jared Diamond's *Guns, Germs & Steel: the Fate of Human Societies*
Jared Diamond's *Collapse: How Societies Choose to Fail or Survive*
E. E. Evans-Pritchard's *Witchcraft, Oracles and Magic Among the Azande*
James Ferguson's *The Anti-Politics Machine*
Clifford Geertz's *The Interpretation of Cultures*
David Graeber's *Debt: the First 5000 Years*
Karen Ho's *Liquidated: An Ethnography of Wall Street*
Geert Hofstede's *Culture's Consequences: Comparing Values, Behaviors, Institutes and Organizations across Nations*
Claude Lévi-Strauss's *Structural Anthropology*
Jay Macleod's *Ain't No Makin' It: Aspirations and Attainment in a Low-Income Neighborhood*
Saba Mahmood's *The Politics of Piety: The Islamic Revival and the Feminist Subject*
Marcel Mauss's *The Gift*

BUSINESS

Jean Lave & Etienne Wenger's *Situated Learning*
Theodore Levitt's *Marketing Myopia*
Burton G. Malkiel's *A Random Walk Down Wall Street*
Douglas McGregor's *The Human Side of Enterprise*
Michael Porter's *Competitive Strategy: Creating and Sustaining Superior Performance*
John Kotter's *Leading Change*
C. K. Prahalad & Gary Hamel's *The Core Competence of the Corporation*

CRIMINOLOGY

Michelle Alexander's *The New Jim Crow: Mass Incarceration in the Age of Colorblindness*
Michael R. Gottfredson & Travis Hirschi's *A General Theory of Crime*
Richard Herrnstein & Charles A. Murray's *The Bell Curve: Intelligence and Class Structure in American Life*
Elizabeth Loftus's *Eyewitness Testimony*
Jay Macleod's *Ain't No Makin' It: Aspirations and Attainment in a Low-Income Neighborhood*
Philip Zimbardo's *The Lucifer Effect*

ECONOMICS

Janet Abu-Lughod's *Before European Hegemony*
Ha-Joon Chang's *Kicking Away the Ladder*
David Brion Davis's *The Problem of Slavery in the Age of Revolution*
Milton Friedman's *The Role of Monetary Policy*
Milton Friedman's *Capitalism and Freedom*
David Graeber's *Debt: the First 5000 Years*
Friedrich Hayek's *The Road to Serfdom*
Karen Ho's *Liquidated: An Ethnography of Wall Street*

The Macat Library By Discipline

John Maynard Keynes's *The General Theory of Employment, Interest and Money*
Charles P. Kindleberger's *Manias, Panics and Crashes*
Robert Lucas's *Why Doesn't Capital Flow from Rich to Poor Countries?*
Burton G. Malkiel's *A Random Walk Down Wall Street*
Thomas Robert Malthus's *An Essay on the Principle of Population*
Karl Marx's *Capital*
Thomas Piketty's *Capital in the Twenty-First Century*
Amartya Sen's *Development as Freedom*
Adam Smith's *The Wealth of Nations*
Nassim Nicholas Taleb's *The Black Swan: The Impact of the Highly Improbable*
Amos Tversky's & Daniel Kahneman's *Judgment under Uncertainty: Heuristics and Biases*
Mahbub Ul Haq's *Reflections on Human Development*
Max Weber's *The Protestant Ethic and the Spirit of Capitalism*

FEMINISM AND GENDER STUDIES

Judith Butler's *Gender Trouble*
Simone De Beauvoir's *The Second Sex*
Michel Foucault's *History of Sexuality*
Betty Friedan's *The Feminine Mystique*
Saba Mahmood's *The Politics of Piety: The Islamic Revival and the Feminist Subject*
Joan Wallach Scott's *Gender and the Politics of History*
Mary Wollstonecraft's *A Vindication of the Rights of Woman*
Virginia Woolf's *A Room of One's Own*

GEOGRAPHY

The Brundtland Report's *Our Common Future*
Rachel Carson's *Silent Spring*
Charles Darwin's *On the Origin of Species*
James Ferguson's *The Anti-Politics Machine*
Jane Jacobs's *The Death and Life of Great American Cities*
James Lovelock's *Gaia: A New Look at Life on Earth*
Amartya Sen's *Development as Freedom*
Mathis Wackernagel & William Rees's *Our Ecological Footprint*

HISTORY

Janet Abu-Lughod's *Before European Hegemony*
Benedict Anderson's *Imagined Communities*
Bernard Bailyn's *The Ideological Origins of the American Revolution*
Hanna Batatu's *The Old Social Classes And The Revolutionary Movements Of Iraq*
Christopher Browning's *Ordinary Men: Reserve Police Batallion 101 and the Final Solution in Poland*
Edmund Burke's *Reflections on the Revolution in France*
William Cronon's *Nature's Metropolis: Chicago And The Great West*
Alfred W. Crosby's *The Columbian Exchange*
Hamid Dabashi's *Iran: A People Interrupted*
David Brion Davis's *The Problem of Slavery in the Age of Revolution*
Nathalie Zemon Davis's *The Return of Martin Guerre*
Jared Diamond's *Guns, Germs & Steel: the Fate of Human Societies*
Frank Dikotter's *Mao's Great Famine*
John W Dower's *War Without Mercy: Race And Power In The Pacific War*
W. E. B. Du Bois's *The Souls of Black Folk*
Richard J. Evans's *In Defence of History*
Lucien Febvre's *The Problem of Unbelief in the 16th Century*
Sheila Fitzpatrick's *Everyday Stalinism*

Eric Foner's *Reconstruction: America's Unfinished Revolution, 1863-1877*
Michel Foucault's *Discipline and Punish*
Michel Foucault's *History of Sexuality*
Francis Fukuyama's *The End of History and the Last Man*
John Lewis Gaddis's *We Now Know: Rethinking Cold War History*
Ernest Gellner's *Nations and Nationalism*
Eugene Genovese's *Roll, Jordan, Roll: The World the Slaves Made*
Carlo Ginzburg's *The Night Battles*
Daniel Goldhagen's *Hitler's Willing Executioners*
Jack Goldstone's *Revolution and Rebellion in the Early Modern World*
Antonio Gramsci's *The Prison Notebooks*
Alexander Hamilton, John Jay & James Madison's *The Federalist Papers*
Christopher Hill's *The World Turned Upside Down*
Carole Hillenbrand's *The Crusades: Islamic Perspectives*
Thomas Hobbes's *Leviathan*
Eric Hobsbawm's *The Age Of Revolution*
John A. Hobson's *Imperialism: A Study*
Albert Hourani's *History of the Arab Peoples*
Samuel P. Huntington's *The Clash of Civilizations and the Remaking of World Order*
C. L. R. James's *The Black Jacobins*
Tony Judt's *Postwar: A History of Europe Since 1945*
Ernst Kantorowicz's *The King's Two Bodies: A Study in Medieval Political Theology*
Paul Kennedy's *The Rise and Fall of the Great Powers*
Ian Kershaw's *The "Hitler Myth": Image and Reality in the Third Reich*
John Maynard Keynes's *The General Theory of Employment, Interest and Money*
Charles P. Kindleberger's *Manias, Panics and Crashes*
Martin Luther King Jr's *Why We Can't Wait*
Henry Kissinger's *World Order: Reflections on the Character of Nations and the Course of History*
Thomas Kuhn's *The Structure of Scientific Revolutions*
Georges Lefebvre's *The Coming of the French Revolution*
John Locke's *Two Treatises of Government*
Niccolò Machiavelli's *The Prince*
Thomas Robert Malthus's *An Essay on the Principle of Population*
Mahmood Mamdani's *Citizen and Subject: Contemporary Africa And The Legacy Of Late Colonialism*
Karl Marx's *Capital*
Stanley Milgram's *Obedience to Authority*
John Stuart Mill's *On Liberty*
Thomas Paine's *Common Sense*
Thomas Paine's *Rights of Man*
Geoffrey Parker's *Global Crisis: War, Climate Change and Catastrophe in the Seventeenth Century*
Jonathan Riley-Smith's *The First Crusade and the Idea of Crusading*
Jean-Jacques Rousseau's *The Social Contract*
Joan Wallach Scott's *Gender and the Politics of History*
Theda Skocpol's *States and Social Revolutions*
Adam Smith's *The Wealth of Nations*
Timothy Snyder's *Bloodlands: Europe Between Hitler and Stalin*
Sun Tzu's *The Art of War*
Keith Thomas's *Religion and the Decline of Magic*
Thucydides's *The History of the Peloponnesian War*
Frederick Jackson Turner's *The Significance of the Frontier in American History*
Odd Arne Westad's *The Global Cold War: Third World Interventions And The Making Of Our Times*

LITERATURE

Chinua Achebe's *An Image of Africa: Racism in Conrad's Heart of Darkness*
Roland Barthes's *Mythologies*
Homi K. Bhabha's *The Location of Culture*
Judith Butler's *Gender Trouble*
Simone De Beauvoir's *The Second Sex*
Ferdinand De Saussure's *Course in General Linguistics*
T. S. Eliot's *The Sacred Wood: Essays on Poetry and Criticism*
Zora Neale Huston's *Characteristics of Negro Expression*
Toni Morrison's *Playing in the Dark: Whiteness in the American Literary Imagination*
Edward Said's *Orientalism*
Gayatri Chakravorty Spivak's *Can the Subaltern Speak?*
Mary Wollstonecraft's *A Vindication of the Rights of Women*
Virginia Woolf's *A Room of One's Own*

PHILOSOPHY

Elizabeth Anscombe's *Modern Moral Philosophy*
Hannah Arendt's *The Human Condition*
Aristotle's *Metaphysics*
Aristotle's *Nicomachean Ethics*
Edmund Gettier's *Is Justified True Belief Knowledge?*
Georg Wilhelm Friedrich Hegel's *Phenomenology of Spirit*
David Hume's *Dialogues Concerning Natural Religion*
David Hume's *The Enquiry for Human Understanding*
Immanuel Kant's *Religion within the Boundaries of Mere Reason*
Immanuel Kant's *Critique of Pure Reason*
Søren Kierkegaard's *The Sickness Unto Death*
Søren Kierkegaard's *Fear and Trembling*
C. S. Lewis's *The Abolition of Man*
Alasdair MacIntyre's *After Virtue*
Marcus Aurelius's *Meditations*
Friedrich Nietzsche's *On the Genealogy of Morality*
Friedrich Nietzsche's *Beyond Good and Evil*
Plato's *Republic*
Plato's *Symposium*
Jean-Jacques Rousseau's *The Social Contract*
Gilbert Ryle's *The Concept of Mind*
Baruch Spinoza's *Ethics*
Sun Tzu's *The Art of War*
Ludwig Wittgenstein's *Philosophical Investigations*

POLITICS

Benedict Anderson's *Imagined Communities*
Aristotle's *Politics*
Bernard Bailyn's *The Ideological Origins of the American Revolution*
Edmund Burke's *Reflections on the Revolution in France*
John C. Calhoun's *A Disquisition on Government*
Ha-Joon Chang's *Kicking Away the Ladder*
Hamid Dabashi's *Iran: A People Interrupted*
Hamid Dabashi's *Theology of Discontent: The Ideological Foundation of the Islamic Revolution in Iran*
Robert Dahl's *Democracy and its Critics*
Robert Dahl's *Who Governs?*
David Brion Davis's *The Problem of Slavery in the Age of Revolution*

Alexis De Tocqueville's *Democracy in America*
James Ferguson's *The Anti-Politics Machine*
Frank Dikotter's *Mao's Great Famine*
Sheila Fitzpatrick's *Everyday Stalinism*
Eric Foner's *Reconstruction: America's Unfinished Revolution, 1863-1877*
Milton Friedman's *Capitalism and Freedom*
Francis Fukuyama's *The End of History and the Last Man*
John Lewis Gaddis's *We Now Know: Rethinking Cold War History*
Ernest Gellner's *Nations and Nationalism*
David Graeber's *Debt: the First 5000 Years*
Antonio Gramsci's *The Prison Notebooks*
Alexander Hamilton, John Jay & James Madison's *The Federalist Papers*
Friedrich Hayek's *The Road to Serfdom*
Christopher Hill's *The World Turned Upside Down*
Thomas Hobbes's *Leviathan*
John A. Hobson's *Imperialism: A Study*
Samuel P. Huntington's *The Clash of Civilizations and the Remaking of World Order*
Tony Judt's *Postwar: A History of Europe Since 1945*
David C. Kang's *China Rising: Peace, Power and Order in East Asia*
Paul Kennedy's *The Rise and Fall of Great Powers*
Robert Keohane's *After Hegemony*
Martin Luther King Jr.'s *Why We Can't Wait*
Henry Kissinger's *World Order: Reflections on the Character of Nations and the Course of History*
John Locke's *Two Treatises of Government*
Niccolò Machiavelli's *The Prince*
Thomas Robert Malthus's *An Essay on the Principle of Population*
Mahmood Mamdani's *Citizen and Subject: Contemporary Africa And The Legacy Of Late Colonialism*
Karl Marx's *Capital*
John Stuart Mill's *On Liberty*
John Stuart Mill's *Utilitarianism*
Hans Morgenthau's *Politics Among Nations*
Thomas Paine's *Common Sense*
Thomas Paine's *Rights of Man*
Thomas Piketty's *Capital in the Twenty-First Century*
Robert D. Putman's *Bowling Alone*
John Rawls's *Theory of Justice*
Jean-Jacques Rousseau's *The Social Contract*
Theda Skocpol's *States and Social Revolutions*
Adam Smith's *The Wealth of Nations*
Sun Tzu's *The Art of War*
Henry David Thoreau's *Civil Disobedience*
Thucydides's *The History of the Peloponnesian War*
Kenneth Waltz's *Theory of International Politics*
Max Weber's *Politics as a Vocation*
Odd Arne Westad's *The Global Cold War: Third World Interventions And The Making Of Our Times*

POSTCOLONIAL STUDIES

Roland Barthes's *Mythologies*
Frantz Fanon's *Black Skin, White Masks*
Homi K. Bhabha's *The Location of Culture*
Gustavo Gutiérrez's *A Theology of Liberation*
Edward Said's *Orientalism*
Gayatri Chakravorty Spivak's *Can the Subaltern Speak?*

PSYCHOLOGY

Gordon Allport's *The Nature of Prejudice*
Alan Baddeley & Graham Hitch's *Aggression: A Social Learning Analysis*
Albert Bandura's *Aggression: A Social Learning Analysis*
Leon Festinger's *A Theory of Cognitive Dissonance*
Sigmund Freud's *The Interpretation of Dreams*
Betty Friedan's *The Feminine Mystique*
Michael R. Gottfredson & Travis Hirschi's *A General Theory of Crime*
Eric Hoffer's *The True Believer: Thoughts on the Nature of Mass Movements*
William James's *Principles of Psychology*
Elizabeth Loftus's *Eyewitness Testimony*
A. H. Maslow's *A Theory of Human Motivation*
Stanley Milgram's *Obedience to Authority*
Steven Pinker's *The Better Angels of Our Nature*
Oliver Sacks's *The Man Who Mistook His Wife For a Hat*
Richard Thaler & Cass Sunstein's *Nudge: Improving Decisions About Health, Wealth and Happiness*
Amos Tversky's *Judgment under Uncertainty: Heuristics and Biases*
Philip Zimbardo's *The Lucifer Effect*

SCIENCE

Rachel Carson's *Silent Spring*
William Cronon's *Nature's Metropolis: Chicago And The Great West*
Alfred W. Crosby's *The Columbian Exchange*
Charles Darwin's *On the Origin of Species*
Richard Dawkin's *The Selfish Gene*
Thomas Kuhn's *The Structure of Scientific Revolutions*
Geoffrey Parker's *Global Crisis: War, Climate Change and Catastrophe in the Seventeenth Century*
Mathis Wackernagel & William Rees's *Our Ecological Footprint*

SOCIOLOGY

Michelle Alexander's *The New Jim Crow: Mass Incarceration in the Age of Colorblindness*
Gordon Allport's *The Nature of Prejudice*
Albert Bandura's *Aggression: A Social Learning Analysis*
Hanna Batatu's *The Old Social Classes And The Revolutionary Movements Of Iraq*
Ha-Joon Chang's *Kicking Away the Ladder*
W. E. B. Du Bois's *The Souls of Black Folk*
Émile Durkheim's *On Suicide*
Frantz Fanon's *Black Skin, White Masks*
Frantz Fanon's *The Wretched of the Earth*
Eric Foner's *Reconstruction: America's Unfinished Revolution, 1863-1877*
Eugene Genovese's *Roll, Jordan, Roll: The World the Slaves Made*
Jack Goldstone's *Revolution and Rebellion in the Early Modern World*
Antonio Gramsci's *The Prison Notebooks*
Richard Herrnstein & Charles A Murray's *The Bell Curve: Intelligence and Class Structure in American Life*
Eric Hoffer's *The True Believer: Thoughts on the Nature of Mass Movements*
Jane Jacobs's *The Death and Life of Great American Cities*
Robert Lucas's *Why Doesn't Capital Flow from Rich to Poor Countries?*
Jay Macleod's *Ain't No Makin' It: Aspirations and Attainment in a Low Income Neighborhood*
Elaine May's *Homeward Bound: American Families in the Cold War Era*
Douglas McGregor's *The Human Side of Enterprise*
C. Wright Mills's *The Sociological Imagination*

Thomas Piketty's *Capital in the Twenty-First Century*
Robert D. Putman's *Bowling Alone*
David Riesman's *The Lonely Crowd: A Study of the Changing American Character*
Edward Said's *Orientalism*
Joan Wallach Scott's *Gender and the Politics of History*
Theda Skocpol's *States and Social Revolutions*
Max Weber's *The Protestant Ethic and the Spirit of Capitalism*

THEOLOGY

Augustine's *Confessions*
Benedict's *Rule of St Benedict*
Gustavo Gutiérrez's *A Theology of Liberation*
Carole Hillenbrand's *The Crusades: Islamic Perspectives*
David Hume's *Dialogues Concerning Natural Religion*
Immanuel Kant's *Religion within the Boundaries of Mere Reason*
Ernst Kantorowicz's *The King's Two Bodies: A Study in Medieval Political Theology*
Søren Kierkegaard's *The Sickness Unto Death*
C. S. Lewis's *The Abolition of Man*
Saba Mahmood's *The Politics of Piety: The Islamic Revival and the Feminist Subjec*t
Baruch Spinoza's *Ethics*
Keith Thomas's *Religion and the Decline of Magic*

COMING SOON

Chris Argyris's *The Individual and the Organisation*
Seyla Benhabib's *The Rights of Others*
Walter Benjamin's *The Work Of Art in the Age of Mechanical Reproduction*
John Berger's *Ways of Seeing*
Pierre Bourdieu's *Outline of a Theory of Practice*
Mary Douglas's *Purity and Danger*
Roland Dworkin's *Taking Rights Seriously*
James G. March's *Exploration and Exploitation in Organisational Learning*
Ikujiro Nonaka's *A Dynamic Theory of Organizational Knowledge Creation*
Griselda Pollock's *Vision and Difference*
Amartya Sen's *Inequality Re-Examined*
Susan Sontag's *On Photography*
Yasser Tabbaa's *The Transformation of Islamic Art*
Ludwig von Mises's *Theory of Money and Credit*

Macat Disciplines

Access the greatest ideas and thinkers across entire disciplines, including

INEQUALITY

Ha-Joon Chang's, *Kicking Away the Ladder*

David Graeber's, *Debt: The First 5000 Years*

Robert E. Lucas's, *Why Doesn't Capital Flow from Rich To Poor Countries?*

Thomas Piketty's, *Capital in the Twenty-First Century*

Amartya Sen's, *Inequality Re-Examined*

Mahbub Ul Haq's, *Reflections on Human Development*

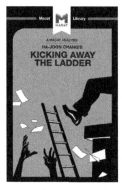  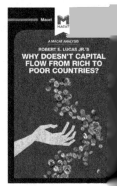

  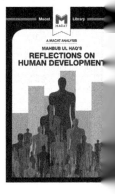

Macat Disciplines
Access the greatest ideas and thinkers across entire disciplines, including

CRIMINOLOGY

Michelle Alexander's
*The New Jim Crow:
Mass Incarceration in the
Age of Colorblindness*

**Michael R. Gottfredson
& Travis Hirschi's**
A General Theory of Crime

Elizabeth Loftus's
Eyewitness Testimony

**Richard Herrnstein
& Charles A. Murray's**
*The Bell Curve: Intelligence and
Class Structure in American Life*

Jay Macleod's
*Ain't No Makin' It:
Aspirations and Attainment in a
Low-Income Neighborhood*

Philip Zimbardo's
The Lucifer Effect

Macat Disciplines

Access the greatest ideas and thinkers across entire disciplines, including

GLOBALIZATION

Arjun Appadurai's, *Modernity at Large: Cultural Dimensions of Globalisation*

James Ferguson's, *The Anti-Politics Machine*

Geert Hofstede's, *Culture's Consequences*

Amartya Sen's, *Development as Freedom*

Printed in the United States
by Bakcr & Taylor Publisher Services